The W
Greatest
Blunders

Clockwise from top left: **aftermath of the 1987 hurricane; the Turin Shroud; the capsized *Herald of Free Enterprise*.**

The World's Greatest Blunders

By
Sue Blackhall

OCTOPUS BOOKS

First published in 1989
by Octopus Books Limited
a division of the Octopus Publishing Group
Michelin House
81 Fulham Road
London SW3 6RB

© Octopus Books Limited 1989

ISBN 0 7064 3901 5

Typeset by Dorchester Typesetting Group Ltd
Printed in Great Britain at The Bath Press, Avon

Contents

Acknowledgements

The publishers would like to thank the following for their kind permission to reproduce the photographs in this book:

Gale Carlill 61

Popperfoto 12, 32, 109, 134, 140, 159/Reuter 128 top and bottom, 153/UPI 76, 144

Rex Features 23 top right, 85, 85 inset, 98

Syndication International 89

Topham Picture Library 23 top left and bottom, 49, 70, 117, 119, 124, 140 inset

Trivial Pursuit 83

Preface

We giggle at gaffes perpetrated by others in light relief that they are not our own. Who would want to be responsible for the hurricane howler of 1987, or to have dropped clangers on the air before an audience of millions? Who would want to be the historian who fell for the hoax Hitler diaries – fakes written on postwar paper – or the US president who told his bewildered Brazilian hosts how pleased he was to be visiting Bolivia – and have the bloomer broadcast world-wide?

When it comes to mistaken identity blunders have more serious, sometimes tragic, consequences and giggles turn to gasps. When heroic endeavour or human error become a matter of life and death we can only mourn the resulting disaster.

Chapter One

SHORTS

This cornucopia of quickfire cock-ups begins with some expensive advertising blunders and a handful of hair-raising motoring stories, in which the 'infernal machine' displays a mind of its own.

As always, the language barrier creates its own confusion and, as this chapter illustrates, certain words just don't mean the same thing in translation!

Bloomers in brief

A top store aimed a sales promotion at their account customers – which included Prince Charles. He received a missive addressed by computer to: Mr. HRH Prince, Charles Buckingham Palace, The Mall.

The letter from the impertinent machine began: 'Dear Mr Prince, what would your neighbours in the Mall think if you pulled up outside Charles Buckingham Palace in a brand new red Ford Fiesta, complete with sunroof and alloy wheels?'

Playing the milkman in a television advert nearly cost British comedian Benny Hill his life. His milk float was meant to disappear as if by magic when his back was turned and a crane was hired to whisk it out of sight.

But as Benny, chosen for the part because of his hit song *Ernie – the Fastest Milkman in the West*, feigned amazement and began to walk back to where the float had been standing, the crane's hook snapped and it crashed to the ground. A few seconds later and Benny would have been the Flattest Milkman in the West.

Worried by the growing number of vegetarians, the U.S. red meat industry fought back with an advertising campaign – but without much luck.

First they used American actress Cybill Shepherd . . . until she confessed she never ate the stuff.

Then they tried showing actor James Garner carving his way through roasts and grills . . . until the celebrity was suddenly rushed to hospital for heart surgery.

At this point, they gave up the idea of using a celebrity to beef up their product. Instead they produced a poster of an all-American boy holding the Stars and Stripes . . . until someone pointed out it was almost identical to an old Nazi recruiting poster.

An international airline advertised its 'rendezvous lounges' in Brazil and discovered, too late, 'rendezvous' is slang for sex in that country.

A baby-food company marketing its product in an African country labelled it with a picture of a cuddly infant.

The population took it literally and boycotted the stuff. They thought the jars contained minced babies!

A 30-second Schweppes advert starring William Franklyn and filmed off the southern coast of Spain turned out to be a costly commercial mistake.

The script called for a desert island but, unable to find one, the admen made their own by piling sandbags on to submerged rocks. They covered the bags with a yellow tarpaulin sprinkled with sand so that it looked like the real, tropical thing.

Rain and gales swept the sandbags out to sea and delayed filming, but finally the commercial was 'in the can'. It showed a marooned Franklyn tossing a tonic water bottle containing a message into the sea. But when it hit the screens, viewers complained it encouraged seashore litterbugs.

The advert had to be taken off after only two flightings.

A canal boat scene for an Andrex toilet tissue advert took almost a year to shoot because of the unpredictable British weather.

For the next commercial, which showed a family sitting on the lawn on a summer's day with the famous puppy romping around them, the ad agency decided to go to California to find the perfect sunny 'English' garden.

But it rained solidly and they had to plant 200 fake daffodils and use floodlights for sunshine.

One of the biggest commercial cockups of all time was the promotion for Strand cigarettes.

Using the slogan 'You're never alone with a Strand', the ads featured actor Trevor Brooke as a lone figure with just his cigarette for company. The public understood this to mean no one would want to know you if you smoked Strand cigarettes.

The haunting theme tune made the music charts and Brooke became a celebrity – but the cigarettes stayed on the shelves.

The brand was withdrawn in 1961, just 18 months after the costly campaign was launched.

Yorkshire viewers were in stitches the night the commercials' soundtracks got mixed up.

The words and pictures went like this:

Voice: 'Clean your teeth with this.'

Picture: A sausage.

Voice: 'Give this to your cat.'

Picture: A bottle of Babycham.

Voice: 'This will make your hair gleam.'
Picture: A tube of toothpaste.
Voice: 'Lubricate your car with this.'
Picture: A bottle of beer.
Voice: 'That's my husband.'
Picture: A contented cat.

In the early days of commercial television, many ads went out live, giving disaster plenty of scope to strike.

One commercial called for a close-up of a slice of Spam covered with mayonnaise. At the very instant the meaty morsel filled the nation's TV screens, a portly bluebottle landed on it, looking, after the admen's magnification, like some hideous monster from outer space.

Barclays Bank bosses blushed when they got their vicars in a twist in a £1,750,000 campaign aimed at newlyweds. The clergyman, shown marrying a young couple, was dressed for burying them, in a black funeral stole!

A clanger in a television commercial was spotted in time to save the Royal Family's blushes.

The ad, for Unipart car spares, was to have asked: 'Do you know how to fit a coil in a Princess?' It had nothing to do with the Royal birth rate. It was advertising a part for an Austin-Rover car.

The Princess in question.

A tea company landed in hot water with a competition designed to boost their teabag sales. It succeeded beyond their wildest dreams. Syndicates devised a way of winning £20 on every box of 160 bags and bought them by the lorryload. One 100-strong London group stood to collect £80,000 for an outlay of £8,600 on 4,000 boxes weighing eight tons.

Their leader explained: 'You had to scratch panels off cards to reveal six hidden teacups. We thought the cards must be quite expensive to print, so that there would be only a limited number of diagrams. We reckoned if we scraped off enough cards we would end up with a key to every diagram in circulation. After that, every card would be a winner. And that's how it worked out.'

There was just one snag. The tea company was prepared to pay out, but its insurers refused, on the grounds that the syndicate competitors had broken the rules by not using their 'skill and judgment'.

Some would argue they had displayed plenty of both.

The Parker pen company in America promised customers they could 'prevent embarrassment' by using a new leak-proof ink.

In Mexico 'embarrassment' was translated as *embarazar* which means 'getting pregnant'. Dealers were besieged by buyers hoping for a new birth control device.

The slogan 'Come Alive with Pepsi' was a huge success in America. But when the company plastered it on poster sites all over Germany the translation read: 'Come alive out of the grave with Pepsi.' Another version proclaimed: 'Pepsi brings your ancestors back from the dead.'

A Lincolnshire man who complained about drivers speeding near his home became the first victim of the radar trap police had set up to catch them.

Angela Harper believed her luck had run out when her van's fan belt snapped on the M6 motorway.

Thinking fast, she took off her tights and used one of the legs as a replacement. It tore as she drove into the next service area, where she bought an emergency belt. A few miles on, that snapped too, and so did the other leg of her tights.

Finally, she slipped off her knickers, and, using them as a frilly fan belt, coaxed her van into Penrith.

'I was beginning to think I'd run out of clothing,' Angela said.

Only then did the 29-year-old driver of Kendal, Cumbria, look in her toolkit . . . and find a spare fan belt.

Lincolnshire businessman Oscar Ejiamike's mistake was to mount a nocturnal expedition to poison moles who were digging up his lawn.

He decided to use the headlights of his XJ4.2 Jaguar to light the scene for his night assault. When the lights dimmed, he started the engine to charge the battery.

Without warning, the automatic car shot backwards and crashed through the wall of his house and into the sitting room, damaging the Jaguar's petrol tank and dislodging a wall-mounted electric heater.

Sparks from the heater ignited the leaking fuel and the car burst into flames. The room was wrecked, the Jaguar gutted, and Oscar's wife Lindy had to flee from the house in her nightclothes.

He spent the next day explaining his £6,000 mistake to the insurance company . . . while the moles carried on undisturbed.

Two Irish roadmen at Hatfield, near Doncaster, made the mistake of trying to save electricity while they had their lunch break.

They switched off the temporary traffic lights at their roadworks on a blind bend. Traffic jammed up for miles until the police arrived to sort out the mess. Said an officer: 'The men felt a bit sheepish when they realized their good deed had gone wrong.'

Drivers who filled up at an Irish filling station found their cars spluttering to a halt after a few yards.

The AA, RAC and police were called out to scores of breakdowns at Lurgan, County Armagh, and discovered the cars had been tanked up with water. The garage had just taken delivery of 'petrol' from a tanker which had been filled up with water to clean it.

No one had remembered to empty it and refill it with the right stuff.

An Exeter AA inspector, called to give a second-hand Mini the once-over, accidentally knocked the automatic gear shift into reverse, and the car went backwards into a brick wall. Then he put it into drive instead of neutral. It hurtled forward into a building. The inspector's call ended up with one written-off small car.

The Japanese Ambassador must have glowed with national pride as he headed for the Birmingham Motor Show to see his country's many exhibits.

But his £20,000 limousine, specially imported from Tokyo, broke down, and he had to wait at a motorway service station for a hired Ford Granada to take him the rest of the way.

Marine engine expert Peter Latham thought fixing his Mini's starting trouble would be child's play.

But three months later, Peter, of Dronfield, Derbyshire, was about to admit defeat. He had spent a fortune on new batteries, chargers, plugs and points. Then he discovered that instead of operating the choke, he had been pulling at the heater control.

An elderly woman was spotted in the loo of a West Country motorway service station trying to dry her hands on the machine next to the wash basin. But no matter how she pushed and pulled the knob, the contraption refused to blow out hot air. 'Thems aren't for drying hands,' she complained.

And she was right. 'Thems' were condom dispensers.

An expensive mechanical advertisement erected by the AA in the Cromwell Road in London showed a three-dimensional front of a car, complete with real steam belching from the grill and hazard lights flashing. A few hours after it was put up, it broke down.

A French doctor driving home to Paris from holiday heard an SOS on his car radio – and realized he had left his wife at a garage 200 miles back. He hadn't realized she had gone to the toilet when he stopped three hours earlier.

'I didn't miss her because we don't talk much while travelling,' he explained.

What's red and yellow, costs £50,000 and won't move?

Answer: A new Irish single-decker bus.

When the Irish State Transport Company took delivery of their new vehicle, the first of a fleet of 50, the transport minister himself took the wheel for a special ceremony.

But the bus wouldn't start. And a change of batteries didn't help to get the vehicle on the road.

And when the minister tried to launch it with Champagne, the bottle simply bounced off the bonnet. At his second attempt, he soaked the mayor of Limerick and injured him with flying glass.

Eventually engineers got the bus moving.

But it broke down a mile away.

American Frank Perkins decided, for reasons best known to himself, to set a new record for squatting at the top of a pole.

Frank, of Los Angeles, earmarked a flagpole in San Jose, California, for his record-beating venture. He was determined to perch there for 400 days.

But life on the ground changed quite a bit while Frank squatted on high. First, the firm sponsoring him went broke. Then his girlfriend went off with another man. When Frank finally made his descent, he found his phone and electricity had been cut off.

That wasn't all. He was still two days short of the world record.

On the day the new station of Sandwell and Dudley, near Birmingham, was opened, a top British Rail official turned up to wait with 30 early-morning passengers for the first train scheduled to stop there.

With a mighty roar, the historic 6.36 am whistled through the station at 70 miles an hour and disappeared into the distance.

No one had thought to tell the driver to stop.

The world of sound should have been music to Mervyn Stoneman's ears. Instead, the 51-year-old printer of Plymouth, Devon, wished he had never had the operation which successfully restored his hearing after a lifetime of silence.

Mervyn had had to wait 10 years for the implant of a special hearing aid, but he realized it was all a mistake when he had to lie awake night after night listening to his wife snoring.

'I often saw her puffing out of the side of her mouth when she was asleep, but I didn't realize she made such a racket,' he said.

Wife Wendy drove him into the spare bedroom with her nocturnal noises. 'He wakes up all the time,' she explained.

She lost out on Mervyn's newly restored hearing too – she could no longer swear at him and get away with it.

Things did not feel quite right when the 81-year-old driver pulled up outside his usual supermarket. The car park seemed to be bigger and emptier then he remembered, and a lot of people seemed to be getting into a flap. What was even more confusing was the sight of a huge aircraft hurtling towards him.

The pensioner had in fact mistaken the airport buildings at Palma, Majorca, for his local supermarket. He had innocently joined a convoy of official cars taking a Spanish government VIP to his plane, thinking it was the usual supermarket car park queue.

Air controllers were speedily alerted to the danger and were able to stop the holiday jet from landing while ground staff hastily redirected the startled shopper to a real supermarket.

When Clara Price was born prematurely, the doctor gave her only two days to live. The frail newborn went on to celebrate her 100th birthday in Newport, Gwent, in October 1988.

Vandals wrecked Northampton pensioner Bob Onn's car . . . while he was giving a talk at a residents' meeting on keeping bored teenagers out of mischief.

An over-enthusiastic police sergeant slapped a parking ticket on a bomber which overshot the runway at RAF Abingdon in Oxfordshire – and fetched up on the roadway.

Chief Superintendent Ken Diccox, head of the Newbury Division of Thames Valley Police, waived the customary £12 parking fine. The sergeant concerned was not named.

The new wine was ready, waiting for the verdict of connoisseur Guy Pelegrin. He climbed a ladder to peer into the vat, lost his balance and fell in. Monsieur Pelegrin, 44, died after being overcome by fumes during the testing of the new grand crû at his home, a castle near Bordeaux, France.

Helpful pensioner Thomas Basil lived to regret his good deed, when he took his wife shopping at the supermarket in Minneapolis, Kansas.

First, Thomas drove into the back of a stationary car, ramming it into the back of another. He immediately pulled over to apologize – and struck another vehicle. His wife, greatly distressed, leapt out of the car. She was run over by her husband.

The shopping trip ended with Mrs Basil in hospital and Thomas heading back home. On the way he drove into an office block.

The owner of a house in Memphis, Tennessee, was shocked when he came home and found the house had been burgled.

Among the debris discarded throughout the house he found his Polaroid camera, complete with a recent picture of a rather startled burglar. The thief had snatched the camera and accidentally taken his own picture, and had forgotten to take the evidence away with him.

The owner took the instant Identikit to the local police and the bungling burglar was arrested soon afterwards.

Newlyweds Sandy and David Ison knew getting married was the right thing for them.

Their honeymoon wasn't.

The brand new Porsche they'd given themselves as a wedding present broke down as they motored through France. It cost them £100 to get it fixed. When they awoke the next morning it had been stolen.

They believed love would conquer all and hired a car to travel further. The car developed gear trouble.

Poor Sandy didn't get to see much of Europe. She was allergic to her wedding ring, and suffered from travel sickness, food poisoning and sunstroke. Enough was enough, the couple decided. They headed for the safety of their home in Oxfordshire, but fate had not finished with them. At Dover, Sandy discovered her purse containing £100 had been stolen.

They eventually made it back to their house, to be woken in the early hours by police reporting that the pet shop they owned had been broken into. David staggered out of bed, went to the shop and discovered a chinchilla had got out of its cage and set off the burglar alarm.

Just as David made it back into bed, there was a real break-in.

The couple never even got to see their holiday photographs. The films went missing.

A British diplomat attending a luncheon party at the American Embassy became involved in an animated discussion with his host.

As he gesticulated to emphasize a point, his arm brushed the head of his hostess, knocking her wig across the room and showing all the world she was completely bald.

Sir Thomas Beecham felt satisfied but exhausted after conducting the Hallé Orchestra in a triumphant performance in Manchester in 1939. He was eager to get to bed after the concert but felt he should linger a little, for the sake of politeness, to greet a woman in the hotel foyer whose face seemed familiar, but whose name he could not for the life of him recall.

They exchanged a few pleasantries and Sir Thomas was about to continue on his way to his room, when something jogged his memory.

'And tell me, how is your dear brother?' Sir Thomas inquired hopefully.

'He is very well, thank you, Sir Thomas,' came the polite reply.

'And what is his business now?'

'Oh, he's still King, you know,' the woman said sweetly.

'A set of traffic lights has been stolen from a main road junction in Exeter. A police spokesman said: "Some thieves will stop at nothing."' – *Exeter Express & Echo*

'Deep freeze meat. Best Scotch meat from Wales.' – *Edinburgh Evening News*

'Why only twelve disciples? Go out and get thousands!' – American movie mogul Samuel Goldwyn

The goose-step, that cocky, strutting march associated with Prussian military precision, was not invented by the Germans. It was introduced by the British Army when a commanding officer created a step which would show him at once if any of his men were drunk.

'English shorthand typist. Efficien. Useless. Apply otherwise.' – Spanish newspaper advert

'To move the cabin, push button of wishing floor. If the cabin shud enter more persons, each one should press number of wishing floor. Driving is then going alphabetically by natural order. Button retaining pressed position shows received command for visiting station.' – Instructions in a Madrid lift

'Hand your baggage to us. We will send it in all directions.' – Advertisement in a Belgian forwarding office

'Erected to the memory of
JOHN PHILIPS
accidentally shot
as a mark of affection
by his brother'
– *tombstone tribute*

Two bickering Frenchmen decided to settle their differences with a duel, but not in the accepted style of the 19th century. They chose to fight with blunderbusses from hot air balloons above the Tuileries gardens.
    Simultaneous shots brought down both balloons, killing both men outright.

You could say David Lloyd George was completely bananas. At the Peace Conference at Versailles in 1919, he came up with the idea that the Italian government should replace commercial losses suffered during the war by increasing banana output. It might have worked – if bananas grew in Italy.

'Raise your glasses and join me in a toast to Prince Charles and Lady Jane.' Businessman Peter Balfour dropped this clanger when he toasted the engagement of the royal couple, in the presence of the then Lady Diana.

It was only after the Duke of Monmouth was beheaded in 1685 for plotting to overthrow King James III that it was discovered an official portrait of the traitor had not been painted.

The powers that be decided to remedy this oversight and ordered the Duke's body to be exhumed. The head was reattached and the body dressed in the Duke's finery so that a formal portrait could be completed.

Gustav III of Sweden believed not only that coffee was bad for you, but that it was poisonous. The Swedish king was so sure of this that he ordered the drinking of coffee as a punishment for a convicted murderer. The killer drank, drank and drank. And lived.

It's not every day a forgetful passenger leaves a fortune in a taxi.

Kevin Butler was behind the wheel of his London mini-cab when he was hailed by Kizoto Idehem, a Nigerian businessman. He wanted to go to a bank to withdraw money and Butler waited patiently while he transacted his business. On his return, Idehem placed a bulging black bag containing £241,000 on the back seat of the taxi. Then the trusting tourist made a costly mistake; he asked Butler to hang on for a moment while he popped into a shop. Butler didn't.

Nothing is too much trouble for the attentive staff of New York's Waldorf Astoria hotel. And when the hotel detective saw a man trip and fall as he made his way downstairs one night, he was there in a flash to assist.

The man's suitcase burst open and out tumbled a load of beautiful jewels. The detective helpfully scooped them all up and discreetly hailed a cab for the wealthy guest. Back at his post the receptionist called to report the theft of more than half a million dollars' worth of gems from one of the rooms.

For a brew that was meant to be mild, it had explosive results. The drink was called Smiles and it certainly put a contented grin on the faces of regulars at a pub in Congresbury, near Bristol. So John Parsons, the landlord of the Old Inn, had a glass himself. It went straight to his head.

Workers at Bristol's Smiles Brewery had accidentally put a 'mild' label on a barrel of their extra strong exhibition ale, 8p more expensive per pint than the mild. Said John, 'By the time we realized the error it was too late. Everyone was either wobbling around with broad grins or snoring in front of the fire. I had to order a fleet of taxis to get them home. Most of the tipplers had pretty thick heads the next morning and one chap couldn't manage to go to work.' But at least the misguided drinkers had value for their money.

Chapter Two

MISTAKEN IDENTITY

The often-tragic results of mistaken identity are explored in this chapter. An innocent man is shot through being in the wrong place and the wrong time, newborn baby girls are muddled up in a Nottingham nursing home and given to the wrong mothers, others are accused of crimes they did not commit, publicly honoured in someone else's place or erroneously reported dead.

Stephen Waldorf

It was 14 January, 1983, the kind of typical winter's evening in London when you have your car heater turned on full. The commuter traffic crawled its way through the city. It was 6 pm, a Friday, and everyone's aim was to get home and put the week's work behind them.

Freelance film editor Stephen Waldorf was sitting in the passenger seat of a bright yellow Mini, stuck in a traffic jam. He chatted amiably with his companions, Sue Stephens and Lester Purdy, who was driving. They idly gazed out of the car window and at the traffic beside them, exchanging indifferent glances with other drivers.

They never realized, for one moment, that they were being stalked, nor that they were the target of an undercover police hunt for a dangerous gunman. They had no idea that their yellow car, inching its way in the heavy traffic, had gunmen's eyes trained on it all the way. Nor could they have known that a desperate alert had been sounded calling crack-shot police officers to spring into action.

The yellow Mini stopped near the junction of Pembroke Road and Earls Court Road, Kensington. Its occupants patiently waited for the traffic to clear. It was then that the shots rang out, like a scene from a TV film drama. A few moments after 6 pm, Stephen Waldorf lay in the seat of the yellow Mini, close to death. It was only after the bloody ambush was over and the streets were cleared of confusion that the crack CID team realized they had made a terrible mistake: they had shot the *wrong man*.

'It was all over in seconds,' said witness Malcolm Hill, who had heard the shots from his home in Pembroke Road. To Hill, it had sounded as if someone was trying to break down his own front door. What he saw, when he cautiously looked out into the street, seemed too incredible to be true. There were two men crouched beside a Mini, one at the front near-side of the car, the other at the back. They both held guns, gripped military-style with both hands and at arm's length. They were motionless, not making a sound. Hill stared in disbelief as several other men ran from behind the car and crouched down in the same position. As onlookers began to approach, a man called out, 'Get away, we're the police.' It was only then that Mr Hill and the other horrified passers-by realized who the 'hit men' really were. Wearing blue sleeveless flak-jackets, not easily noticed in the dark, the police team looked like gunmen who had found their prey.

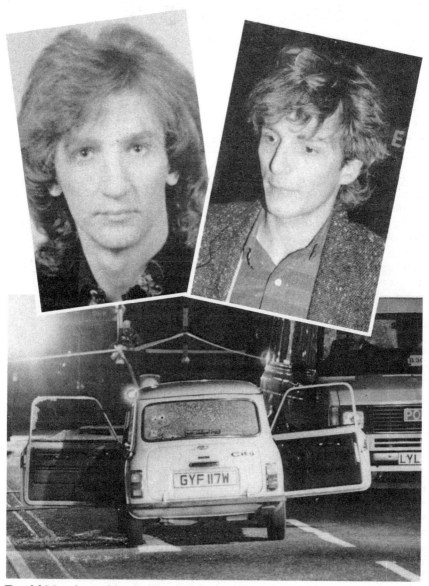

David Martin and lookalike Stephen Waldorf; the shot-out mini.

MISTAKEN IDENTITY

By this time, both doors of the Mini were wide open; the passenger seat was empty. 'At first, I didn't realize there was a girl in the back,' continued Hill. 'There was no sound coming from the car and I think she must have crouched down.'

The policeman at the front of the car knocked out the window of the passenger door using the butt of his gun, as if to get a better view. He then immediately reverted to his original stance, with the gun held in both hands and out in front of him, while, 'very slowly and deliberately', more policemen approached the car. Little did they know that neither the driver, Lester Purdy, nor the man they had shot, Stephen Waldorf, was the killer they were after.

For the top officers who were hunting hardened criminal David Martin, it was all a tragic fiasco. Martin, aged thirty-five, had escaped from a cell at Marlborough Street Magistrates Court on Christmas Eve 1982, where he was awaiting trial on charges of attempted murder of a police officer, possession of a firearm and other charges, including one concerning a £25,000 bank robbery. Martin was a police-hating gunman, who would shoot if approached. He had to be caught.

That night, CID officers had been convinced they had spotted Martin in the yellow Mini. When the Mini stopped, they had decided to make their move, fearing their target might soon be swallowed up in the rush-hour flow of traffic. They knew they could not afford to take any chances; they had to get their man. But they made a near-fatal error, and when the shooting had died down, it was Stephen Waldorf – not David Martin – who slumped out of the car door.

Amazingly, Stephen's fellow passengers, Sue Stephens and Lester Purdy, escaped serious injury. Purdy ran 'petrified' into the night, through a hail of police bullets. But the real miracle was that Stephen Waldorf escaped death. His body was riddled with bullets. One had entered him just above the right hip, narrowly missing his spine and nerve cord, on one side, and the aorta (the main body artery) on the other. Had the bullet hit the spine, Stephen would probably have been paralysed for the rest of his life; had it hit the aorta, it would almost certainly have killed him. There were also bullet wounds in Stephen's shoulder and thigh, and there were cracks in his skull. Stephen was lucky not to have suffered brain damage.

The speed and expertise of surgeons and nursing staff at London's St Stephen's Hospital saved Stephen's life, but it was a twenty-five-year-old off-duty nurse, Jane Lamprill, to whom much of the credit was due. Jane had heard the commotion from her house just 20 feet away from where the shoot-out occurred. It was she who bandaged his arm and held a dressing to his chest until he arrived at the hospital. Doctors said later her actions had been vital in saving the young man's life.

While Stephen lay in agony in Pembroke Road, questions were already being asked: Why had an innocent motorist been gunned down? Scotland Yard began to give its side of the story. According to the police, one of their team had shot the left-hand rear tyre of the Mini to stop it from moving off. This single shot was followed by a barrage of perhaps 13 others, which shattered the windows of the car and severely wounded Stephen. Perhaps, they said, the very first shot had been mistaken by their team as having come from somebody inside the Mini.

The Yard wanted to emphasize that a police team on an operation as dangerous as the hunt for David Martin would consist of highly trained men who were primed to react instantly. Perhaps it was because of this that the gunmen acted without restraint.

The police had a detailed description of the man they were looking for. Martin, a known bisexual, had blond hair and a distinctive hooked nose. It was also known he sometimes disguised himself as a woman, complete with stockings, and that he got some kind of kick from tucking a gun into his suspenders.

Stephen Waldorf bore only a slight facial similarity to Martin, but there the physical similarities ended.

There was, however, one link. Sue Stephens, his fellow passenger that night, was David Martin's former girlfriend. Police had already staked out the flat in Hampstead which she shared with a girl friend. They had kept watch over Christmas, hoping Martin, on the run and with few friends, would try to make contact with her.

After the shooting, Sue Stephens, falsely claiming she, too, had been hit by a bullet, was handcuffed and taken away by police and interviewed at Kensington police station, only a hundred yards away from the ambush.

Her flatmate was also brought in for questioning. Later, both Sue Stephens and Lester Purdy were charged and jailed for handling stolen goods for Martin. At the trial it was stated that some of the stolen items had been found in a flat once occupied by Stephen Waldorf. Stephen, however, denied that he had ever met Martin.

In October 1983, two of the detectives involved in the ambush, Constables John Jardine and Peter Finch, were acquitted at the Old Bailey of attempting to murder Stephen Waldorf and of wounding him. Although disciplinary charges were brought, Mr Jardine was quietly posted to the Yard's Criminal Intelligence branch and Mr Finch returned to uniformed duty.

The one acknowledgment that something had gone drastically wrong that January night, was that neither of the two constables was permitted to carry guns again.

Stephen, who had been struck by five bullets and suffered head injuries, made a miraculous recovery. He fought back from the brink of death and was in hospital for six weeks. It was an extraordinary recovery, said Mr Hoile, the surgeon leading the team at St Stephen's. Emergency treatment had included calling in doctors from another hospital, the Brompton Chest Hospital, to drain one of Stephen's blood-filled lungs. His life had hung by a thread for four days and nights. Then he was able to breathe without a ventilator.

Five days after the shooting he was eating solid food. One week later he could actually get out of bed and sit in a chair. And even talk.

In February 1984, Stephen was awarded nearly £150,000 compensation by Scotland Yard. It was, they admitted, a disastrous blunder on that bitter January night. But they also argued that Stephen may have placed himself in jeopardy by associating with friends of David Martin. Said Stephen as he picked up the cheque: 'I suppose it is a fair sum. But nothing could really compensate for the horrors I went through. I thought I was going to die.'

Months after the shooting he admitted he still suffered horrific nightmares. In them he saw guns pointed at him and flashes.

'Sometimes I wake up in a cold sweat shouting "No, No don't shoot." I believe I am back in that car with the police firing at me.' He also said he bore no grudge against the police who shot him. 'I hold no bitterness against them as individuals.'

It was the system, he said, that was to blame.

And he had no harsh feelings about Constables Jardine and Finch not being jailed. 'Like me they will have to live through that nightmare. I will never forget what happened but nor will the gun cops.'

WHAT JUSTICE FOR THE HUNTED MAN?

David Martin was jailed in October 1983. He was found guilty of shooting at a policeman and of firearms offences. The sentence was 25 years in prison.

Martin had been caught 35 days after he escaped police custody. His former girlfriend Sue Stephens had tipped off Scotland Yard. Martin went on a hunger strike and took an overdose in an attempt to get his ex-lover to see him in jail. She refused.

On Tuesday, 14 March, 1984, David Martin hung himself in his cell at Parkhurst Prison on the Isle of Wight. A prison officer had looked in on him just moments before.

The yellow Mini, a colourful but macabre exhibit, kept in police custody in case it was required during the court hearing, was put up for sale. But only when its bodywork was repaired of bullet holes.

The case of the nursery mix-up

From the moment a baby draws its first breath, any mother can tell her newborn's cry from a roomful of other fractious infants, and any mother knows at once that the tiny bundle in her arms could belong to no one else. This makes the tale of the mixed–up babies one of the most heart-rending cases of mistaken identity.

The story of the tragic tots goes back to a crisp autumn night in Nottingham in the 1930s. No one believed Margaret Wheeler when she told them the newborn baby they had given her to hold was not hers. Margaret's own baby daughter, delivered at term on November 18, 1936, was longer, thinner – and redder.

The newborn baby Margaret was handed by a nurse soon after she had given birth was quite different. It was a girl, but there the similarity ended. This baby was obviously premature; Margaret noticed the little nails were not fully developed.

In distress, she summoned another nurse and other medical staff, but they scoffed at her claim. No hospital in the world would make a mistake like that.

'But I'd seen my own baby in the delivery room,' Margaret recalled years later. 'The baby they gave me when I got back to the ward had clearly been born early.'

She was right. The infant had been born six weeks prematurely to Margaret's ward neighbour, Blanche Rylatt. The two women had given birth at almost the same time.

Margaret, having failed to convince the hospital that she had been given the wrong baby, approached Blanche in anguish. But Blanche refused to consider the possibility that a hospital could be so seriously at fault and Margaret had to watch distraught as another woman cuddled and nursed a baby girl that she herself had borne.

It was in great distress that Margaret left the Nottingham nursing home with a child she firmly believed belonged to another woman. She tried gallantly to wipe her doubts from her mind and for seven years gave the little girl all the love a mother could bestow on her offspring. But the

27

terrible conviction that the little girl she was nurturing was not hers continued to fester.

Eventually Margaret mustered all her courage and went to see Blanche again. She suggested that they should go back to the hospital to look at the birth records so that they could be sure, once and for all, that nothing had gone wrong.

By this time, the women shared a close, if somewhat strained friendship. Each little girl called her mother's friend 'aunt' – and it was uncanny how much they resembled their aunties.

Blanche agreed to what she considered a rather unnecessary check, but she was shocked when she and Margaret returned to the Nottingham nursing home they had left seven years before with their babies. They were allowed to examine records. No one could argue with what had been written in black and white. It was clear the babies had been swapped.

The wrong doctors' names were on the forms; notes of the labour, medication given, and the time of birth of each baby related to the wrong mother! Blood and saliva tests proved conclusively what Margaret had tried to tell medical staff all those years before.

The baby blunder was bad enough, but the decision Margaret and Blanche made afterwards was even more dramatic. They agreed they would carry on bringing up each other's daughters. Little Peggy, Margaret's daughter, was to be raised by Blanche and her husband Fred, while Valerie, Blanche's daughter, would continue to be cared for by Margaret and her husband Charles.

The mothers decided not to tell Peggy and Valerie the truth, but agreed to keep in touch. That meant each mother could lovingly monitor her own daughter's growing-up, even though she had no part in it.

It was a touching pact, made because both women thought it would be too disruptive for the children to be taken from the homes they considered theirs.

'We agreed, on counsel's advice, that the children should stay as they were,' said Margaret.

For a while, Margaret was deeply upset by the heart-rending decision she had made. She admitted there was a time when she wanted both children – a desire also experienced by Blanche.

It was only a matter of time before the little girls would grow into intelligent young women, and eye their mothers and 'aunts' suspiciously.

Peggy is now 51, but she still remembers the first moment she started wondering about her parents. She was about 10 and stared longingly at her 'father's' hands, wondering why she hadn't inherited his slender fingers. She couldn't help noticing that Blanche and Fred were both slim, fair-haired and blue-eyed, while Peggy was a brunette, brown-eyed, and, in her own words, 'large and gawky'.

'I was always puzzled by how different I was from my parents,' she said.

Eight years later she found the courage to express her doubts. She was now a junior civil servant. Her 'Aunt Margaret' and 'Uncle Charles' had popped in to see her as she sat munching her sandwiches on Nottingham Castle green one lunch hour. The couple paid regular visits from their home in Cumbria.

'Aunty Margaret showed me a photograph of her other daughter, Denise, born three years after me. I looked at it and then at her.

'I simply said, "You're my mother aren't you?"'

The truth was finally out. Both Margaret and Blanche were relieved, because it had been inevitable and because it had come from one of the girls themselves.

For Peggy, many mysteries were solved that day. 'The likeness of that photograph was incredible. I just knew Denise was my sister. It cleared up all the things I had been puzzling over for years.'

Valerie was told the truth while on a course at a teacher training college. When she qualified she had to say a painful 'goodbye' to Margaret and Charles and begin to pick up the pieces of a new life with her real parents, Blanche and Fred.

'I'll never forget the moment when I opened the little gate that led to the path to the front door or the feeling of waiting for that door to open,' she recalls.

For Margaret and Blanche, all those years of living a lie were over. But they still feel, as only mothers can, that what they did was the right thing for their children. Peggy and Valerie are both married and each has two children of her own, which has made it easier for them to understand that tragic decision. Valerie lives in Andorra with her two youngsters. Peggy lives in Nottingham, with her family. The two women consider themselves sisters, and are as close as real sisters could be. The muddled-up babies harbour no resentment for their 'lost' teenage years.

For Margaret, now 79, and Blanche, now 74, mother love finally won through. Blanche often thinks back to that moment in a Nottingham nursing home, when she was asked by a nurse, holding Valerie: 'Is this baby yours?'

Catching up with the Joneses

Having the same surname as thousands of others can bring problems enough. But one luckless woman, Susan Jones, also shared her christian name, date of birth and home town with someone else – and ended up in court as a result.

Susan Jones's troubles began when she returned to her home in Barnsley and found a police squad car waiting for her.

An officer handed her a summons to Bristol magistrates' court to face a charge of owning a dangerous dog, which had viciously bitten a woman. There was another charge of keeping two dogs without a licence. The charges related to offences allegedly committed in Bristol 18 months previously. Susan Jones knew it couldn't possibly have anything to do with her. She'd lived in Barnsley for six years, had never been to Bristol in her life and the only dog she'd ever owned was a little Jack Russell that had died the year before.

But Susan Jones had not reckoned with the determination of the boys in blue. To them it was a fair cop. The more she protested her innocence, the more the police insisted she was the person they were after. They suggested she wrote to the court. Susan did as they suggested but received no reply. She telephoned – and was told to put her complaint in writing!

The only response was a letter saying the date of her hearing had been changed, and warning that the case would go on if she didn't turn up.

By this time, pregnant Susan was in great distress. 'That was when I broke down and cried,' she said.

Two months after her ordeal began, she was found 'innocent'. The prosecution explained that police had answered a complaint from a woman who had been badly bitten by a dog, and found its owner, another Mrs Susan Jones, had moved to Barnsley.

Susan eventually received an apology from the chief superintendent of Avon and Somerset Constabulary, admitting their 'regrettable error'. What cleared Susan's name in the end? She was working in a shirt factory in her home town on the day she was supposed to have been in Bristol. Her employers confirmed it. And the police went on the Jones hunt again.

Tragic coincidence

By tragic coincidence, the two girls who were injured in a bad car crash near Seville in Spain looked remarkably similar. One girl later died. The other, terribly scarred and with facial injuries which made her virtually unrecognizable, lived, but suffered from loss of memory as a result of the accident.

The parents of the one girl were grief-stricken and went into deep mourning, while the other couple prepared themselves for the long fight to help their daughter to get back to normal. As she recovered, the sickening truth dawned on them – she was not their daughter. In the confusion of the accident, the hospital had mixed up the girls' handbags, and, as a result, their identification.

Two months after the crash in 1978, the grieving family were re-united with the daughter they thought they had lost. The patience and love of the other family turned to despair when they learnt they had been nursing someone else's daughter – and it was theirs who had been buried.

Heinous errors

There were celebrations all round when, in 1976, Young Liberals' president Peter Hain was acquitted of a robbery. The case was widely publicized because it hinged on a question of identity.

Peter Hain, charged with stealing £490 from Barclays Bank in Putney, West London, was picked out in an identity parade. Hain strenuously denied the charge, but three of four schoolboys who saw the chase after the robbery were convinced they had seen him, and at a police identity parade four days after the incident on 24 October, 1975, cashier Lucy Haines pointed him out.

An unjustly charged Peter Hain.

It took an Old Bailey jury four hours and 55 minutes to bring in a verdict of 'not guilty' on 9 April, 1976. Hain's wife Pat and his family were naturally overjoyed at the acquittal which ended months of speculation and suffering.

'I feel absolutely insulted and degraded that even one person could think I might have been a thief,' Hain said after his acquittal. But he was one of the luckier ones.

He escaped being jailed for a crime he did not commit.

In December 1974, an innocent man was offered £17,500 compensation after spending five years in prison. It was the largest pay out ever for someone jailed in error.

The victim, Laszlo Virag of Windsor, Berkshire, had been wrongly accused of stealing parking meter coin boxes in Bristol and Liverpool, shooting and wounding a police officer and resisting arrest. He was convicted by a jury at Gloucester Assizes and sentenced to ten years at Parkhurst prison.

Virag, a 35-year-old Hungarian, was identified by several policemen and other witnesses, but he maintained he was in London, 130 miles from Bristol, at the time of the alleged offences.

Nine witnesses had testified to this at his trial.

Later, another man was found to have used the gun involved in the case.

Electrician Alphonso Eric Douglas, 30, spent 36 days in custody in 1977 for a crime he did not commit. He was also pointed out at an identity parade. Douglas was accused of an £8,750 armed robbery.

Said Douglas: 'I don't think it is right that a person should be charged on just identification evidence alone. I think there should be other evidence. The past six months have been a nightmare for me and my family with these terrible charges hanging over my head.'

In March 1968, lorry driver Albert Chapman was released after 17 days behind bars at Leeds prison. Chapman, 33, won freedom for a crime he didn't commit, after a confession from the real villain, Roy Roberts, 25. The two men were similar in appearance.

Chapman was jailed for nine months at Bradford Quarter Sessions after being wrongfully convicted of driving a van while knowing it to be stolen and for assaulting a police officer. His conviction rested on his identification by Bradford PC David Hemsley. Roy Roberts was in prison for other offences when he heard of the mistake, and confessed.

The lorry driver later went to see Roberts' wife, Maureen, so that she could pass on his thanks. 'If he hadn't owned up, I'd still be in jail,' he told Maureen.

Yet another case of criminal mistaken identity involved 41-year-old Leonard Everington, a labourer of Ipswich, Suffolk. He spent four weeks in prison awaiting trial on three theft charges.

He was discharged at Ipswich Quarter Sessions when Mr William Howard QC said: 'This case illustrates the dangers of identification through photographs alone.'

Everington, charged with stealing from Ipswich churches, had in fact confessed to the crimes. He had done so, he said, 'under pressure'.

Two men who did not confess after being wrongly identified still had their freedom taken away from them. Both cases occurred in 1968.

Harry Wimpress, 60, a night watchman, was alleged to have attacked a nurse and stolen her handbag. He was picked out at an identity parade by another nurse, but a stranger, Francis Holden, 20, owned up after Wimpress had spent 21 hours in a cell.

Patrick Crundal, 20, a shop assistant, was alleged to have stolen bank notes from women in Bradford. Six women identified him in court as the one who had nicked their money.

This time, 17-year-old Jeremiah Delaney owned up, but only after Patrick had spent four weeks in custody. They were said to look alike.

The strangest case of mistaken identity must be that of a man accused of a street robbery which took place while he was in a police station to report that he had been assaulted!

William McRoberts, 37, spent seven weeks in jail because of an amazing mix-up. It happened like this. A Mr Kenneth Jennings was attacked by four men and robbed of £10 at Victoria Station in London.

At that moment, McRoberts was at his local police station in Sutton, Surrey, telling police how *he* had just been assaulted.

A few nights later, McRoberts was at Victoria Station, when Jennings saw him and mistook him for one of his previous assailants. He called the police and McRoberts was arrested.

Unfortunately, he couldn't at first remember exactly where he had been at the time of the four-man attack. Eventually, and luckily for him, he did. From behind bars he sent a message to his solicitor. A police sergeant from Sutton went to Brixton Prison and confirmed McRoberts' alibi.

The one-minute beauty

It was the moment every beauty queen dreams of, when her name is announced as the glamorous golden girl – the winner.

Beautiful blonde Sharron Gardiner of Cardiff was overjoyed to be acclaimed as Miss Wales in the Miss World heat in 1987.

Her glory lasted just one minute. Sharron, 23, was walking up to be crowned, applause ringing in her ears after being told she had won the contest at Pontypridd Municipal Hall in Mid Glamorgan, when the bad news was broken by Miss World chairman Eric Morley. He hastily explained that there had been a mix-up in the scrutineer's count. The real winner was 18-year-old Nicola Davies from Merthyr Tydfil who won £2,000 and a holiday in Greece. She would also go on to represent Wales in that year's Miss Universe contest in Singapore.

Said Sharron's father: 'It was a terrible blow. She has been taking part in beauty contests since she was 15. Representing Wales in the Miss Universe contest was to be the pinnacle of her career. She put everything into preparing for it.'

Eric Morley did give Sharron £1,000 compensation for her disappointment. 'I was handed a piece of paper. When I announced the result the scrutineer suddenly realized he had made a mistake, ran across and gave me the right result,' he said.

Sharron accepted her consolation prize philosophically.

'At least I can say I was Miss Wales, if only for a minute. I felt so humiliated. I don't think I'll ever enter a competition again,' she commented sadly.

The spy who stayed out in the cold

The spy who fooled the world made history and hit the headlines as a hero before his cover was finally blown – by his own brother.

Everyone knew of Charles Henry Evans, Britain's wartime master spy who had infiltrated the Nazi hierarchy. He even had the temerity to write to intelligence expert and author Nigel West to correct his references to MI6 in a book, and he brazenly took part in a BBC-TV news interview, his face half-hidden behind a venetian blind to protect his identity.

The world heard how Evans had been recruited into MI6 while still at Marlborough public school, had studied medicine at Heidelberg University and had later adopted a German identity. He described how he became a colonel in German Military Intelligence and went on to win an Iron Cross, all the while busily feeding Nazi secrets to Britain.

It was all too much for his brother Gerald, who decided to speak up in 1985 after a blaze of publicity.

Charles did not go to Marlborough, but to Kilburn Lane High School in North London, he declared. He was never involved with MI6, nor was he a doctor. He had been a ship's trainee purser, an office clerk and a pub barman.

Gerald conceded that Charles had seen service – as a dispatch rider in the British Army. And his contact with the enemy took place when, as a humble private, he was captured in France and spent five years as a prisoner of war in camps in Poland.

'The only gong he got was his service medal from the British Army,' Gerald said. 'And he must have been exhausted coming home to Paddington every night when he was supposedly studying medicine in Germany.'

Charles needed medical help, Gerald stated.

But one fact of the bogus spy's amazing life story was true, or nearly true. It appeared he had been to Marlborough – to buy an old school tie for a friend.

After these family revelations, Charles Henry Evans did not dare to come in from the cold.

Grave error

A graveside funeral service was held up for half an hour when the vicar realized he was burying the wrong body. He noticed, as wreaths were removed from the coffin top, that it bore a man's name – and not that of great-grandmother Nora Boote.

Relatives waited in the church while embarrassed funeral directors rushed off to collect Mrs Boote's body and coffin so that the service at St Michael's Church in Bishops Hitchington, Warwickshire, could continue.

Dead or alive?

Ethel Clunas faced a heart-breaking task. She had been called by the police to identify her son, killed in a climbing accident in Scotland. She had been shocked to read about the fatal accident in the newspapers. Police could put no name to the body two other climbers had found in the Cairngorm foothills in Scotland. Ethel noted the age of the unidentified victim, about 25, his description, and the fact he was wearing a gold Timex watch with a brown leather strap.

Her heart sank. It had to be her son Stephen.

She travelled from her home in Inverness to make the formal identification. Yes, she confessed in tears, it was Stephen. The grief-stricken family went through the harrowing ordeal of registering the death and making funeral arrangements. Then Stephen rang to say hello.

Ethel had identified a complete stranger as her son.

The sad tale turned to overwhelming relief because a family friend had read about Stephen's 'death'. Pat Harvey thought it strange that Stephen's body could have been found on a Saturday, when she had chatted to him in Aviemore the day after. Pat, who used to work with Stephen in the laundry department of a local hospital, knew for certain she couldn't be mistaken. 'I told the police that if Stephen was dead I must have just had tea with a ghost,' she said.

Police paid the Clunas family another visit, then Stephen's brother-in-law Fraser Ross and his father Angus went to the mortuary to see for themselves. This did not help to clear up the confusion for the now distraught family.

Said Ross: 'I thought it was Stephen although I was not sure because people change after they die. But his father thought so too.'

Police at Inverness had to step in. They took fingerprints from Stephen's home and matched them with the corpse's. They were not the same. They scoured hotels around Aviemore after hearing Stephen had been staying there and finally found him – alive and well.

Said Stephen: 'I am glad to be back home but I did not know anything was wrong until the police contacted me. I tried to phone home but couldn't get through.'

'It has been an awful shock,' Angus Clunas said. 'One day our boy was dead, the next he was alive. It was like having him brought back from the dead.'

It had all been an amazing but tragic coincidence. The clothing on the body made Ethel Clunas sure it was her son. The face was remarkably similar and so was the hairstyle. Later, happily reunited with her son, she said: 'This has been a terrible mix-up. You would have to have gone through what I have to know how I feel.'

Identical twins

Identical twins Simon and Peter Eubanks had Sussex police seeing double. Simon, 26, a professional boxer, was charged with theft from a Brighton store. But the case was withdrawn when no one could be sure which brother had actually turned up in court.

Simon had denied the charge and prosecutor Trevor Small thought it unwise to proceed. Peter Eubanks was also a professional boxer.

Crash victim

The life support system for teenage car crash victim Kristine Bailer was turned off – on the orders of another girl's parents.

The couple's own daughter, Wendy Liby, was killed outright in the same accident in Fort Wayne, Indiana. Kristine was critically injured.

Officials confused the names of the two victims and mistakenly called Kristine's friend's parents to ask for permission to switch off the life support system. They gave it.

Spitting image

Wherever he went, the little boy was treated like Royalty. Children would beg their parents to be allowed to say 'hello'. Grown-ups stood aside, looking on in awe. It was not everyday, they all thought, you clapped eyes on the future King of England. Only it was not the eight-year-old Prince Charles.

Way back in 1957, the right royal recognition caused a big problem for proud mum Mrs Betty Shepherd. Her son Martyn was the spitting image of the little prince. They were the same age, had the same shy smile and wore their hair parted in the same way. Naturally, the similarities caused confusion.

When Mrs Shepherd and her husband took Martyn to a hotel in Sussex the hotel owner promptly called the local police to report his fears that Prince Charles had been kidnapped.

The constable who turned up took a lot of persuading that Martyn Shepherd was not a Royal kidnap victim.

'Since he was six months old people said how closely he resembled the Prince,' said Mrs Shepherd. 'Children in parks ask their parents if they can speak to the Prince.'

The similarity for the Shepherds, who lived in Morden, Surrey, did not end there. When Charles got flu, Martyn had a temperature too. Mrs Shepherd had a curious theory about her son. She believed that her great interest in the Royals, especially the Queen, could have influenced Martyn's looks. 'I read everything I can about the Royal Family. If Martyn misbehaves, I tell him Prince Charles wouldn't do that.' Martyn would sometimes reply: 'I bet he would!'

Said Mrs Shepherd: 'He's proud of being like the Prince and although he's so young he seems to have the feeling that he has something to live up to. I want him to show the same fine, sturdy qualities that we see in Charles,' she went on. 'But if he got conceited we'd stop it very quickly.'

Boeing horror

In a tragic air crash, a Boeing 727 struck a mountain in northern Cyprus, killing 15 people – and causing unnecessarily prolonged anguish to the families of the three air hostesses who perished.

British crew Andrea Pegg, 23, of Bournemouth, and Sharon Simcock, 29, of Blackpool, worked for the Turkish airline Talya whose flight was on its way to Nicosia when the plane crashed. Sharon's body was not returned to Britain, because it was mistaken for that of a Turkish air hostess and buried in a communal grave in Istanbul. Andrea's corpse was sent in error to a Blackpool mortuary, where Sharon's body should have been sent. And the horrifying mix-up was complicated further when the body of Turkish air hostess Mensah Banu was thought to be that of Andrea and was sent to the British girl's home town of Bournemouth.

The mistake came to light only when RAF pathologist Wing Commander Ian Hill noticed the dental records of Miss Banu did not match those of Miss Pegg. He travelled to Blackpool to make the correct identification while officials in Istanbul faced the terrible task of exhuming Andrea's body.

'The only forms of identification on the crash victims were plastic adhesive labels,' the pathologist reported. 'The whole business should have been carried out by people who knew what they were doing.'

Chapter Three

AGAINST ALL ODDS

This chapter contains some of the most embarrassing moments in history. Burglars who do nothing but bungle, intimate amorous adventures that suddenly become public performances and experts who seem to attract disaster create the kind of unbelievable situations recounted in these pages, which seem to occur against all odds.

Don't count on it

Derek Howell paid £85,000 for a newsagent's shop in Hastings, Sussex, just to have access to the parking space for his Rolls-Royce. Then he discovered his £40,000 pride and joy was too wide to fit it.

Customers were delighted with the bonus they received from a cash dispenser at a New York bank. A cashier had put 20 dollar bills in the five dollar slot and card holders got four times what they asked for. No one got away with it though. Their names had all been recorded with their transactions.

Father of two Matt Casey hit the roof when he received his building society statement, claiming he owed nearly £1 million on his three-bedroom semi in Washington, Tyne and Wear. A computer hiccup had sent similar letters to more than 200 customers of the Northern Rock Building Society.

Two guard dogs worth £350 were stolen from the house they were supposed to be protecting in Whaplode Drove, Lincolnshire. Their owner, Rosemary Cormack, said: 'We hoped the dogs would scare people off.'

A Swiss bank desperately offered a £2,000 reward to trace a lucky customer who had been paid out £46,000 by mistake. A girl cashier had confused Austrian schillings with German marks which are worth twice as much. She rushed after the customer but he vanished in the crowds.

The bungling bandit was as blind as a bat without his glasses, and that was how he came to make a spectacle of himself. He decided a disguise was called for when he went to rob a jeweller's shop and put on a new suit and a false beard for the occasion, but left off his specs. The myopic marauder burst into the shop, snatched a tray of rings and ran off – smack into a parked car just outside. Staff at the shop in Brighton, Sussex, soon overpowered the confused thief.

A Durham museum hurriedly removed a Roman coin from display when a little boy spotted it was a free plastic token from a soft-drink company.

A mugger thought he was on to a winner when he tackled a betting shop worker carrying two plastic bags. He was able to snatch only one, and made off down the road with his takings. When he felt safe, he took a look at his haul and found he had stolen a bag of dirty washing. The day's takings from the shop were in the other bag.

Inventor Lieutenant Ivan Saevas was awarded 40,000 dollars for designing a training device that saved the Swedish Air Force nearly eight million dollars. First the tax authorities took 30,000 dollars off Saevas then they decided he was now in a higher tax bracket so deducted another seven thousand dollars.

Finally they said he was liable to social security and other taxes so demanded 16,000 dollars more. Saevas was left 13,000 dollars worse off after inventing the money-saving device. The tax people said they would investigate his case.

The parents of Anton Grellier were sorry they ever called him stupid. When he grew up and became a wealthy Belgian businessman, Grellier sent them generous cheques – incorrectly made out so they couldn't be cashed.

Once bitten . . .

When farmer Lawrence Littley went muckspreading, he was a little too generous and caused quite a stink.

Littley forgot to turn off his sprayer as he towed it home behind his tractor – and coated the picture-postcard village of Musbury, Devon, with a layer of evil-smelling sludge. In his sound-proofed cab, the farmer was unaware of the chaos he left in his wake as he showered fertilizer on eight cars, seven houses, several angry locals and the post office.

The blunder would have been embarrassing for anyone, but especially so for Littley, who was chairman of the local parish council. That night the red-faced farmer went back to the village to clean it up.

Escapologist Eric Ward finally had to admit defeat – in a British Rail toilet. One of Eric's tricks was to be chained in a straight-jacket, then hauled 100 feet up on a rope by a crane. The rope would be set alight and Eric would be out of the jacket and on to the crane in seconds.

Another feat consisted of his being tied to the frame of an advancing circular saw and freeing himself before he could be sliced up.

But he was helpless when the lavatory lock jammed on an inter-city express taking him from London to Stoke-on-Trent.

Said Eric, 39, of Woking, Surrey: 'It was the most embarrassing moment of my life and I was hoping to keep it quiet. I tried every trick I knew but the lock wouldn't budge.'

The escapologist was still trapped when the train left Stoke. His ordeal lasted an hour before his knocking and cries for help were heard.

A director filming a river scene for a television commercial wanted to include a group of ducks, but they kept swimming out of the picture – until someone had the bright idea of anchoring them with bricks and lengths of string tied to their legs. The admen decided to move upstream to a better location, taking the co-operative ducks with them, but the new stretch of water was deeper and the string too short.

Weighted down by their bricks, the poor ducks sank. As one adman, the entire crew dived in and rescued them.

When Joseph Begley of Evesham, Worcestershire, sent off 2,000 cigarette coupons for a watch, nothing happened. He wrote to complain, and within three days, 10 parcels had arrived from the cigarette company. The next day there were 18. The next day, 10 more. By this time, Begley had received three tape recorders, a golf bag, a pressure cooker, two electric blankets, a baby's cot, a doll and many other things he didn't really want. Running out of space, he asked the company to stop sending him gifts. They replied – with a letter of apology and 10,000 coupons to make up for his inconvenience.

He sent them off, ordering tools and a bedspread. By return came two ladders and a plant stand.

Mr Begley swapped his brand of cigarettes.

The picture decorating the lids of tins of biscuits for the Christmas market showed a colourful scene of an old-fashioned tea party in an English country garden – just the thing to give to granny with a bottle of sherry. But if granny had good eyesight, she would have choked on her sherry and custard cream. Just a step away from the elegant ladies pictured sipping their tea, two terrier dogs were busy engaging in something very rude and across the lawn could be seen the naked limbs of a couple seeking more excitement than tea and biscuits.

Thousands of the tins had gone out to the shops before a Middlesex grocer spotted the saucy scenes. Huntley and Palmers, who made the biscuits, said it must have been an agency artist's idea of a joke and scrapped the remaining stock at a great loss.

Every newspaper takes pains to prevent it, but sometimes the same item is published twice. *The Scotsman* seems to have gone one better. An Edinburgh reader wrote this letter to the editor. 'Sir, I note with interest that you have published my letter of 13 June three times (so far) this week. I'm pleased that you like it so much but if the letter is to become a regular feature in *The Scotsman* I'd appreciate a small fee by way of acknowledgement. May I add that I approve of your use of different headings each time the letter is published. This stops it becoming too stale or repetitive. Let me know if your readers grow tired of the letter and I'll send you a fresh one.'

Reluctant soldier Peter Lenz of Nuremberg, West Germany, thought he had the perfect ruse for dodging call-up. He went for his medical with a urine sample from his girlfriend, a diabetic. But a few days later, Peter received orders to report for duty. A covering letter said: 'We would have believed you were a diabetic – but not that you are pregnant.'

Would-be worshippers dialling London's Westminster Abbey for times of services were taken aback by an angry female voice saying: 'It hasn't come out yet. Sod it.' Hundreds of callers heard the unholy slip, made by the receptionist who recorded the tapes for the answering machine, but no one at the Abbey noticed for two days.

An Abbey spokesman said: 'She was trying to record a message when several people were demanding attention at the reception desk and phone calls were flooding in. She suffered acute embarrassment afterwards and was in a state of near collapse. But the clergy have heard much worse language. They took a light-hearted view of it.' Showing true Christian tolerance, they forgave the red-faced receptionist.

Shipbuilders scratched their heads when they surveyed their latest bit of work on a nuclear submarine. Something didn't look quite right. Then the awful truth dawned. They had welded a large section upside down! A senior union member of Vickers in Barrow, Cumbria, described the mis-match as a 'monumental cock-up'. The mistake is thought to have happened when a section of the vessel arrived without proper identification. Workers had to re-weld the part. Ironically, the submarine was named *Triumph*. 'It was very embarrassing,' said a Vickers spokesman, and declined to say what the mistake cost the taxpayer.

Jumble sale organizer Judith Fraser-Smith was floored when she realized she'd sold off the local town hall carpet by mistake. The carpet was kept in Bakewell Town Hall, Derbyshire, and unrolled only to deaden the sound of footsteps when the magistrates' court was sitting. Members of St Giles's Church in the Peak District village of Great Longstone had taken it thinking it was jumble. Judith contacted her helpers but no one knew the young couple who'd made the £1 bargain buy. A notice was pinned outside the church hall and an advert placed in the local newspaper. A week later the couple rang to say it was they who had the town hall carpet, and they'd cut it up to fit their staircase.

The man from the ministry was just explaining why he didn't consider a notorious blackspot dangerous. But his firm words: 'I will not accept that this is a highly dangerous road' were interrupted by three cars piling up behind him. Jim Davidson from the Ministry of Transport carried on talking as first a blue estate car in the background ran off the road and up a steep grassy slope, followed by a screech of brakes as the second car, swerving to avoid the estate, smashed into the back of another vehicle. The whole scene was captured on TV and broadcast to millions of ITN early evening news viewers. Mr Davidson's crash course took place when he visited the A19 near Peterlee, Durham.

Nadine Williams of 13 Newall Crescent, Fitzwilliam, West Yorkshire, was delighted with her new bathroom. She thought it was a birthday surprise from her husband. But he knew nothing about it. Plumbers should have called at Number 30 Newall Crescent. By the time they realized their mistake they had ripped out the Williams's old bath, wrenched off the wall tiles and completed the £450 renovations.

Passengers on a Britannia Airways flight from Zurich to Gatwick listened in horror as a stewardess announced the plane was about to ditch in the sea. She explained the emergency procedure, as white-faced passengers listened in terrified silence for two minutes.

Then the voice of the captain came over the intercom. 'It was a mistake. We were meant to tell you we were about to serve the duty frees.' The wrong pre-recorded tape had been played.

The binmen's blood ran cold when they heard a baby crying inside their dustcart. Driver Stan Anderson, horrified that someone could dump an infant, immediately called his council depot boss Alex Patterson who said: 'Search the lot.' The refuse team at Luton, Bedfordshire, tipped five tons of rubbish out into the street and frantically began their mercy hunt.

After clawing through mountains of garbage, they found the crying child – it was a talking doll. The toy's battery had somehow been switched on when it landed in the back of the cart. Said Mr Patterson: 'The cries were incredibly life-like and it gave the men a real scare.'

Irishman Brendan Murphy, 25, was caught on the hop when he raided a shoe shop in Bedford. He swopped his worn-out training shoes for a classy £29 pair of cowboy boots. But staff had no trouble spotting him when he tried to make a getaway, wearing two right boots, one a size nine, and the other a size 11. Murphy was put on probation by the town's magistrates.

Love on the rocks

Britain's oldest married couple in 1988, Ted and Florrie Bradley, postponed their 100th birthday parties when they discovered they were both only 96.

For Karen Bowen, it seemed a naughty but nice way to end a fun evening out at a nightclub in Windsor, Berkshire. The tall, dark, handsome and obviously wealthy stranger invited her back to his luxurious home, to romp in a whirlpool bath and on a king-sized bed. When Karen woke the next morning her Romeo had gone. The three people staring at her were the estate agent and two prospective buyers of the show house.

Newlyweds Kenneth and Donna Kiehn posed for just one more picture at their wedding reception – and fell off the balcony to crash down 30 feet into an indoor fountain. 'They were still holding hands when we pulled them out,' said a friend.

A Californian couple decided to spice up their sex life. They checked into a Santa Barbara hotel for seven days of fun and frolics – which they videoed and replayed endlessly. They couldn't understand why the staff gave them flowers and champagne and the manager halved their bill when they checked out. Then they learnt their home movies had accidentally been transmitted all over the hotel, entertaining staff and guests.

Engineers were baffled by a real-life Agatha Christie mystery on the Orient Express. They were called in because the train refused to budge when the stationmaster waved it off at Innsbruck station in Austria on its Paris-Venice run. They began working through the train . . . and found the cause of the trouble in the very last compartment. A young couple making love were blissfully unaware that the girl's foot had become entangled in the communication cord, automatically jamming on the brakes.

A London publisher took his mistress to Normandy, leaving his wife under the impression that he had been called away to Brussels on business. The sneaky pair spent a blissful week together in an olde-world hotel, soaked up the sun and wined, dined and loved in fine style. They returned home, convinced that their sexy secret would never come to light.

A year later the publisher, perhaps with a pang of conscience, took his wife to a travel agent to arrange a holiday for just the two of them. Browsing through the brochures, she came upon one extolling Normandy as the place to unwind. The cover showed a happy, laughing couple leaning against a harbour wall with their arms around each other, unaware that they were being photographed by the French Tourist Board. It was the erring husband and his girlfriend.

A police hunt for an IRA bomb suspect netted a cheating husband. He had told his wife he was going fishing but went away with a girlfriend instead. He sparked off a security alert while tucked up with his lady love, for he had left his car parked outside the Grand Hotel in Brighton, the target of IRA bombing in 1984.

Police became suspicious, found the car owner's name and address in Wiltshire and rang his wife. She said he couldn't possibly be in Brighton, but in Dorset fishing with friends.

This alarmed the police even more. They sealed off the hotel, a helicopter hovered and sniffer dogs were sent in. The two-timing husband and his lady arrived in the middle of it all. They were taken away and questioned but later released. 'He'll be entering another sensitive area when he gets home,' a policeman remarked wryly.

The sensitive zone that exposed a two-timing husband.

Suah Shaheen was looking forward to her wedding night with new husband Mohamed Saleh. Not until it was too late did she find out he was really a 'she', married to a man, and with two children of her own. Police were called and had to break the news that Saleh, 29, liked to wear men's clothes. The registrar who had conducted the marriage ceremony was arrested. Police said he should have noticed!

The woman boss of a West German building firm refused to pay a £130 fine for speeding in her BMW, insisting it was a company car and anyone of 16 staff could have been driving it. Miffed at having their word doubted, the police sent photographs taken by their radar equipment to her home. The snaps showed her doing 86 miles an hour, with a young man nuzzling up close to her as she sped along. Her husband declared that he was to divorce her and would use the snaps as evidence. The attentive boyfriend faced a charge of endangering road safety.

When Zaza Kimmont returned to her New York home after a holiday she found a strange toothbrush next to her husband's in the bathroom. There were traces of lipstick on the bristles. Zaza was furious. Convinced there was another woman, she angrily smashed up the home, shattering lamps, china, vases and ornaments, gouging furniture and slashing paintings. She stormed back home to mother . . . where she learned the truth. Her husband had invited his mother to stay while she was away, and the toothbrush belonged to her. The insurance company refused to pay out for the thousands of dollars' deliberate damage to the apartment.

A seven-year-old boy living on a top-security base near Ipswich, Suffolk, dialled 999 and said his parents were having a terrible fight in the next room. Military police stormed in and found a red-faced mum and dad making love not war.

The earth moved for a courting couple parked on the beach at Weston-super-Mare, Avon, when their car began sinking in the sand. A garage recovery vehicle sent to pull them out also got stuck. Then a second rescue truck got bogged down. All three were hauled out the following day by four vehicles linked together.

A pair who got overheated in the snow started a full-scale emergency alert when an old lady saw a pair of legs sticking out of a snowdrift under a hedge. She ran to the nearby post office and said she had found a body. A 999 call went out and police and ambulancemen raced to the field at

Nuneaton, Warwickshire – and flushed out a young couple who leapt up and ran off naked, clutching their clothes. Police described the lovers as 'cool customers'.

Two teenagers kissing in a car at traffic lights in Rio de Janeiro held up traffic for two and a half hours when their dental braces became entangled.

In Sicily, 64-year-old Duke Giuseppe Avarna made sure everyone knew when he was making love to his beautiful 29-year-old girlfriend . . . by having the village church bells rung. But sleepy locals did not appreciate the nightly ding-dongs. The Duke was fined £15 for disturbing the peace and £70 for 'insulting' his estranged wife. His lawyers said: 'He is crazy about his girl and wants the entire dukedom to share his happiness.'

A sexy secretary's search for Mr Nice Guy attracted far more male attention than she had expected, when a letter she had written to a friend found its way to government and newspaper offices throughout Canada.

The love-lorn secretary had dictated her desires into a computerized office printer at the state government offices in Quebec, and the machine, which could not tell the difference between official and private correspondence, immediately sent copies to every member of the government, the press, and all the other secretaries.

They were bemused to read the memo which said: 'My love life is a bit dull. I haven't seen him for two weeks. Men, they're not easy to understand. Tell me if you meet a nice, good-looking guy. I'd be happy to meet him. Solitude is a heavy burden.'

'It was a technical error,' said Jacques St Onge, the woman's departmental head.

It's criminal

A man handed a bank cashier in Del Ray Beach, Florida a badly spelt note reading: 'I got a bum. I can blow you sky height.' The cashier showed it to his colleagues and they all fell about laughing. The would-be raider was so embarrassed he ran away.

After robbing a garage in Reno, Nevada, a gunman allowed the owner to make just one phone call. He did – to the police.

Robbers used too much explosive on a bank safe in Munkebo, Denmark, and demolished the building. When they finally managed to crawl out they found the safe, still intact.

A burglar unwittingly became an advertisement for a security equipment firm he raided in South London. An infra-red device detected his body heat and set alarm bells ringing. Police arrested him within two minutes.

Finding his victim had no cash, an Essex mugger forced him to write a cheque. 'My name is Andrew Cross. Make it out to me,' he ordered. His victim promptly went to the police, armed with the name of his assailant.

A policeman was amazed when a thief waved at him from the Bristol shop he was burgling. The crook had mistaken the policeman for his accomplice.

A burglar broke into what he thought was a block of flats and found himself in the lap of the law, in Knightsbridge Magistrates' Court, London.

Hoping to cut his electricity bills, a County Tyrone man tampered with his meter. But he fiddled it in the electricity board's favour, and clocked up thousands of extra units and a £600 bill.

A burglar planning to raid an off-licence broke into the wrong shop, took nothing, was arrested within minutes and suffered the indignity of a judge telling him: 'Give up crime, you're no good at it.'

Two raiders out to rob a Buckinghamshire post office tricked the postmistress into opening the security window by asking her to change two £50 notes. She snatched their money and slammed the window shut and they fled empty-handed – and £100 worse off.

Police soon caught up with a thieving motorist who drove off from a Midlands petrol station without paying – and spluttered to a halt less than a mile up the road. He phoned the AA who diagnosed the problem. He had filled up with diesel fuel instead of petrol.

Two handcuffed prisoners leapt from a prison van in Luton, Bedfordshire, and made a dash for freedom. But the shackled pair were stopped short when they ran past a lamp-post, one on either side of it. They were yanked off their feet, collided in mid-air and crashed to the ground in agony. They were rushed to hospital with dislocated arms and crushed ribs.

Two lovers running drugs for a gang discussed their mission as they cuddled in a Worcestershire hotel room – not realizing the baby alarm was on and everything they said was being broadcast to the reception desk. The desk receptionist promptly called the police.

Three prisoners from Lincoln were hitching a lift when a bus stopped for them – and out jumped seven warders from their jail who recaptured them. The warders were escorting a group of prisoners to court.

The 75 convicts who tunnelled out of jail at Saltillo in northern Mexico slipped up on the planning. After six months of hard digging for freedom, they emerged in the nearby courtroom where most of them had been sentenced.

Forgers are often caught by their printing mistakes. But a Kenyan crook who produced near-perfect banknotes was easily identified, thanks to his vanity. Instead of a portrait of the president, he used a picture of himself.

When a would-be robber pushed a note demanding cash across the counter of a wine shop in Yorkshire, shopkeeper John Patterson had to laugh. Neatly printed at the top was the man's name, address and postcode. When the thief produced what appeared to be a gun in a handkerchief, Patterson pelted him with sweets from a jar, then chased him out of the shop armed with a bottle of Coke. Detectives caught up with the hapless thief less than an hour later.

An Irish thief broke into a London electrical shop to steal television sets, but drove off with three microwave ovens by mistake. In court, the judge suspended the man's 18-month jail sentence because of his 'crass stupidity'.

Richard Richardson barged to the front of the queue in a Texas bank and shouted: 'This is a stick-up. Give me the money!' The 20-year-old cashier retorted firmly: 'You're in the wrong line. Wait over there.' Richardson meekly waited – until the police turned up.

An Oregon bank robber pushed a note to the cashier reading: 'This is a hold-up and I've got a gun. Put all the money in a paper bag.' After reading the note, the cashier wrote on it: 'I don't have a paper bag.' The thwarted thief walked out shaking his head.

Nothing went right when an Italian decided to rob a bank in Milan. He tripped on a door mat as he burst in and fell. His mask dropped and his revolver went off. He got up, ran towards a cashier, slipped and grabbed the counter for support, dropping his gun. With staff and customers laughing, he rushed out humiliated – straight into the arms of a policeman who was writing him a parking ticket.

A cool Southampton crook strolled into a city supermarket and filled a basket with goods. He went to the checkout and gave the cashier a £10 note, intending to snatch the contents of the till when she opened it. But the till contained only £4.37, which he took, losing £5.63 on his robbery.

Tourist traps

A pretty girl on holiday from London was admiring the grand pre-Revolution buildings of Red Square in Moscow when a fur-hatted comrade sidled up to her. Furtively he pressed a note scribbled in Russian into her hand. It was, she was sure, a top-secret message for British Intelligence that she had to guard with her life. Her heart pounded as she passed through security checks at Moscow airport, but her secret remained undiscovered and, back home, she took it straight away to London University to be translated. The note read: 'You ugly English cows are all the same.'

A woman asked for a refund on her new passport at Reigate, Surrey. She was unhappy, she told post office staff, because she'd discovered the Lake District was not in Holland.

It's easy to forget something when you're packing for a holiday. And housewife Susan Grove of Cheshire forgot her birth control pills. She remembered as she and her husband, with their baby daughter, were heading for Dover to catch the cross-Channel ferry, and they pulled off the motorway to visit a chemist's. While they were away from their car, it was stolen, complete with their luggage and £800 spending money. They spent the next fortnight at home – gardening.

A German couple sunbathing nude on a beach at Tropea, Italy, were arrested under a bylaw which allows bare bottoms only if they meet 'the highest standards of classical beauty'.

A British Rail guide to scenic railways in Devon had cover pictures of Selworthy village, which is in Somerset, and cannot be reached by train.

Publican John Weller snapped away enthusiastically on his holiday in Yugoslavia. But back home in Long Whatton, Nottinghamshire, he was shattered when his prints arrived. He had 24 perfect shots of his left ear. 'I must have held the camera the wrong way round,' he said sheepishly.

It was the height of embarrassment for British Airways when they flew their beauty queen Kim Turner to Cyprus to promote their image. As Kim, 23, landed safely at Nicosia, her luggage was being expertly unloaded at Zurich. Her suitcases, containing her uniform and cocktail dresses vital for her six-day tour, reached her a day later.

Expertease

Builder Stan Gordon spent a day bricking up a doorway, stood back to admire a job well done – and still didn't spot his mistake. He had walled himself in. Red-faced Stan of Daventry, Northants, discovered the blunder when he tried to leave. There was another door, but it was locked. He finally escaped after shouting for help to a shop assistant across the road.

Workmen were called in to improve security at a Birmingham block of flats for the elderly. They were told to fit entryphones so that callers could identify themselves. But the workmen installed them on the inside of the doors and no one could get in.

A builder's blunder at a new jail on the Spanish island of Ibiza made it easy for prisoners to escape. He put in cell door locks which could only be opened from the inside. The prisoners had to promise on their honour not to escape.

Builders of a new primary school at Taunton, Somerset, made a glaring error when they put clear glass in the lavatory doors. Parents helped replace the glass so that the school could open as scheduled in September 1984.

There was a bigger problem with the loos at Northamptonshire County Council's new nuclear fall-out shelter. It didn't have any. Officials controlling emergency services would have to risk radiation by nipping outside to spend a penny.

A house taken over by Channel 4 for a do-it-yourself series was left in an unlettable condition by the television experts who renovated it. Inspectors from Milton Keynes Development Corporation gave the semi the thumbs down after the series *Anything We Can Do* ended. A spokesman said: 'It looked great on television, but not if you had to live in it.'

Firemen at Barnsley, Yorkshire, had faces as red as their engines when magistrates refused to issue a 10-year registration certificate for their new social club. It had no fire escape.

Equally embarrassed was the senior London Transport engineer who took the first £50,000 bus of a new fleet on a test run . . . and tried to drive the 20 foot double-decker under a 13 foot bridge, slicing the entire top off the vehicle. The only injury was to the driver's pride.

Demolition experts sometimes blow it too. Like the Irishman and his pals who were demolishing a pier at Greenock, Strathclyde. They had to be rescued by an RAF helicopter because they had started work from the wrong end.

A team at Reutte, Austria, blew up the wrong railway bridge – the new £1 million structure that had been opened only three days before.

A demolition team turned up at the home of Barbara Worthington in Cheshire. She arrived back from shopping to see them tearing her place down. They had come to the right street – and the right number. It was the town they got wrong. The workmen should have been knocking down 54 Brookside Avenue, Poynton, but instead, they set to work smashing up the same address at nearby Offerton.

When a Swiss hotel chef lost a finger in a meat-cutting machine, he submitted an insurance claim. The company, suspecting negligence, sent an expert to see for himself. He tried the machine out to prove it was safe – and lost a finger too. The chef's claim was approved.

To check whether curtains in a hotel ballroom were flame resistant, a Vienna fire prevention officer held a lighter to them. He thought he had safely extinguished the fire that resulted, but minutes after he had left, the room was ablaze, ruining the stage, valuable paintings and part of the roof – and no doubt the fire officer's reputation.

The head of the Royal National Lifeboat Institute museum at Bristol capsized while out sailing. A lifeboat was sent to rescue him.

A man in Rochester, New York, cancelled all engagements while his three-day bout of hiccups lasted. 'They're kinda embarrassing in my line of business,' he said. He was area director of the National Council on Alcoholism.

An Irish contact lens manufacturer was awarded £45,000 damages when he walked through the glass door of a golf club, injuring himself badly.

Soon after qualifying as Britain's first woman train driver, Anne Winter had her first crash . . . when the miniature steam engine she was driving at an Oxfordshire school fete came off the rails at three miles an hour. Organizers discovered it was caused by children leaning out and a blushing Anne said: 'Thank heavens it wasn't my fault.'

Electrical expert Phil Sunderland was covered in confusion after getting his wires crossed on BBC breakfast television. Viewers jammed the switch-board when he connected the live wire to the earth pin while demonstrating his firm's new plug.

Within minutes, presenter Selina Scott warned viewers not to make the same dangerous mistake but to leave it to the experts.

A group of Harwich lifeboat men who hired a boat to go on a river trip with their families ran aground on mud flats. They had to be rescued by their own lifeboat manned by a reserve crew.

Dr Yvonne Hodges was delighted to find she was unexpectedly expecting a baby . . . and embarrassed too. She ran a family planning clinic near her home in Axminster, Devon. Yvonne and her husband – also a doctor – declined to confess which birth control method had failed them.

A policeman's lot

Policeman Jimmy Landels will never forget the first time he locked someone in his shiny new handcuffs. It was his grandmother, and he had to send for the police to free her.

Jimmy, 19, was on holiday at home in Brora, Sutherland, after graduating from police college. His 77-year-old grandmother asked him how the handcuffs worked and he proudly demonstrated – on her. Then he realized he had left the key at Inverness, 75 miles away.

He said: 'I had to phone the local police for help, but granny saw the funny side and sat there laughing until tears came to her eyes.'

There were red faces all round when Warwickshire policeman Eric Clegg, on holiday with his wife in Sorrento, Italy, had a visit from the local police. They accused him of spending forged currency.

The fake cash had been handed to him in error by his bank back home, who swiftly wired out new funds.

WPC Fenella Whitehouse made an arresting sight as she ran naked from her house to chase a suspect. Fenella, 20, likes to sleep in the nude and when she heard someone trying to break in, she jumped out of bed and chased the intruder.

'It was only when I started running through the garden that it dawned on me I was starkers,' she said later.

Fenella failed to get her man, but male colleagues from her Bristol police station caught up with him later.

It was an embarrassed pair of bobbies who took their brand new Panda car back to the station at Slough, Berkshire, with £200 worth of damage.

They had been ordered to catch up with three men driving a stolen dumper truck, and they soon spotted it chugging along at 10 mph. Just like the telly cops, they roared past and blocked the road. The villains jumped off and ran, with the two constables in hot pursuit. Meanwhile the dumper truck continued on its slow but steady course – slap into the back of the police car.

Nottingham detectives who had handcuffed a youth to the wheel of their car while they chased his friends returned to find their captive – and the car – gone. It was later found abandoned, with the handcuffs still attached to the wheel.

Then there was the blushing bobby who got lost on his own beat. Teasing colleagues nicknamed him The Mole because he was unable to find his way out of a network of subways in Birmingham. He was too embarrassed to radio for help or ask passersby for directions, and was eventually rescued by a search party.

Puffing runners in a half-marathon near Kirkcudbright wished they'd never seen the motor-cycle cop who escorted them. He took a wrong turning and the 10 leading runners behind him lost their chances of winning. They ran 19 miles instead of 13.

Another 60 behind them in the race clocked up an extra two miles before realizing they were on the wrong road.

59

Sometimes, police blunders call for real teamwork. Crack cops swung into action when a passerby spotted a safe dumped by the road. One man stood guard, detectives took fingerprints, and a Land-Rover arrived to carry it back to the station at Halesowen, West Midlands.

But try as they might, the burly bobbies just couldn't shift the thing. That was when they realized it was a junction box – firmly cemented to the ground.

Two policewomen in South Yorkshire are still trying to live down the day they took two prisoners by mistake – on a goodwill visit to a school. Julie Marshall and Jackie Lawrence let two youngsters handcuff themselves together, and found they didn't have a key to release the boys. They had to take the 12 year olds back to the station to be freed.

A traffic experiment for police in Bristol had embarrassing results too. Rush-hour traffic was found to flow more smoothly after police point-duty had ended.

When a sharp-eyed officer spotted a valuable stolen car in a South London side street, it was taken to the police station. But when fingerprint experts went to examine the £18,000, 150 mph Cosworth Sierra, it had been nicked again – from the garage behind the station.

The light-fingered talents of an arrested burglar got one cop out of trouble. When a PC drove up with the criminal, the duty sergeant at Preston police station went outside to open up the garage for him – and the station's door slammed shut behind him. With no key and no idea how to beat the sophisticated electronic security system, the two cops had to ask the burglar to open the door. He did so in just a few seconds.

An officer alone in the police station at Tuffley, Gloucestershire, locked himself in the loo, and had to radio for help on his walkie-talkie.

But policemen have their human side, as this tale shows. A lady driver pulled up at traffic lights in Hampstead, London, followed by a male driver and, behind him, a police car. As the lights changed, the lady moved away and then stalled.

The man behind her braked sharply and gave an angry blast on his horn. Whereupon the policeman behind him switched on his loudhailer and said: 'Come along sir, give the lady a chance.' By now very flustered, the woman driver started off again – and stalled once more.

Cops came unstuck trying to take a junction box into safe-keeping.

Back in the police car, someone had forgotten to switch off the loudhailer. An amplified groan was heard booming through the street: 'Silly cow's done it again!'

Security-conscious police towed away cars parked near a Glasgow hospital during a visit by Princess Margaret and left them in side streets. When the owners finally managed to track their vehicles down they found 'helpful' notes on the windscreens from a Sergeant Collins telling them where to find their cars.

And when prisoners escaped by helicopter from Gartree jail, police set up road blocks to catch them.

In a police campaign against car tax dodgers in Barnsley, Yorkshire, most of their own patrol cars were nicked for having out-of-date licences.

PC Graham Markwick lectured schoolchildren at Deal, Kent, on how to foil bike thieves and advised them to get their bicycles stamped with their postcode . . . then found his own had been stolen. It wasn't stamped.

In Salford, Manchester, 70 officers made a dawn swoop on a 13th-floor flat, rifles at the ready. But it was the wrong address. The two escaped convicts they were seeking got clean away from a neighbouring tower block.

It's not just British policemen who sometimes end up with red faces. Two New York officers who stepped out of their squad car to investigate suspicious loiterers on a river pier heard the crunch of wheels on gravel as the group fled.

They turned round just in time to see their car rolling forward and plunging into the water. They had to catch a bus back to their station.

Two women agents from FBI headquarters in New York were sitting in Central Park when they were set upon by muggers who took their jewellery, cash and guns before leaving them handcuffed to each other with their own handcuffs.

Star-spangled clangers

Jackie Onassis became the golden girl of the literary world when she persuaded millionaire popstar Michael Jackson to write his autobiography for her employers, Doubleday publishers.

It was a publishing coup, because 'Wacko Jacko' rarely gives interviews at all, let alone baring his soul for a book. Surprisingly, the whole deal went off without a hitch.

Alas, poor Jackie was not so successful with other sign-ups. Having failed to persuade the elusive Hollywood legend Greta Garbo to write her memoirs, she turned her attention to another big name – sultry Italian star Sophia Loren.

Jackie sent an assistant to the home of the sex goddess in Lucerne, Switzerland. Would La Loren, the aide asked, write her autobiography – including her 'extraordinary love affairs and marriages'.

Sophia was not interested – but came up with a suggestion of her own. 'Tell Mrs Onassis to write a book about *her* extraordinary love affairs and marriages,' she retorted.

British television presenter Selina Scott will never forget the night she dropped one clanger after another in the presence of hundreds of VIPs.

By the time she'd finished presenting the Salute to the Falklands Task Force concert, she was wishing the ground would swallow her up. She had announced actor Denholm Elliot as Donald Sinden, another distinguished thespian; actor Richard Todd became Sir John Mills; and English rose Virginia McKenna was confused with Dame Anna Neagle.

Blonde TV action girl Anneka Rice hit the wrong note when she interviewed guest trumpeter Herb Miller on ITV's TV-am programme.

'Between your legs you have something to show us,' she said cheekily. Herb, brother of famous Glenn, burst out laughing at the saucy gaffe.

Sports presenter Jimmy Hill was worried about pronouncing the tongue-twisting name of a rugby player, Nigel Starmer-Smith. Before he went on air, he repeated the name over and over again to get it right.

On air Jimmy pronounced the player's name perfectly, and overcome with relief continued: 'He had seven craps as scum-half for England.'

Important officials waited in vain for Mastermind general knowledge quiz host Magnus Magnusson to turn up to open a restored windmill. The man with all the questions came up with the answer – he had completely forgotten about it.

Magnusson, who had been invited in his capacity as chairman of the Ancient Monuments Board, and had even plugged the event, at Nithsdale, Dumfriesshire, on radio, confessed afterwards: 'I just forgot.'

Sometimes a star learns the hard way that if you say the wrong thing it's best to move on to another subject. British comedian Michael Bentine was watching an audition for a stage show. After listening to the woman singer on stage, he turned to the man next to him and said: 'Isn't that awful?'

'That's my wife,' his neighbour replied.

Trying to salvage the embarrassing blunder, Bentine pressed on: 'I didn't mean the singer. I meant the song.'

'I wrote it,' came the reply.

Former motor-racing champion James Hunt was delighted to be invited to the launch of a new Mercedes model. The ace took it on a 100 miles an hour demonstration lap before an audience of motoring journalists, experts and Mercedes executives at Donington Park.

He handled the speedy vehicle with all the skill you would expect from an ace driver. Well, nearly all. Unfortunately he had forgotten to take the handbrake off and brought the gleaming £20,000 machine back to the pits with smoke pouring from the wheels.

The public likes to see the famous falter – and they got value for money from American TV announcer Ben Graver.

After an orchestral concert, he told millions of viewers: 'You have been listening to the New York Symphony Orchestra under the baton of Atosco Touranini . . . I beg your pardon, Otosco Tiscani . . . I mean Artuto Toscanni.'

Eventually he gave up and started again: 'Your announcer has been Ben Graver, ladies and gentlemen. Remember the name. You may never hear it again.'

But delighted viewers phoned in their hundreds, demanding that he should not be fired. He wasn't.

On the cards

Fate really put the boot in for the Wellington family. They won £100,000 in a football draw – but lost the prizewinning tickets.

John, Sally, and their son Mark, 19, could have kicked themselves when they realized they had misunderstood the rules. Mark had been given a ticket showing a picture of Liverpool star Ian Rush when he filled up with petrol at a garage taking part in the football game. To stand a chance of winning a fortune, Mark had to match his card up with another showing Liverpool's club motif, and they actually had the matching card in their home in Parragate, Cinderford, Gloucestershire. But the Wellingtons all thought they had to have two pictures on one card to win. So they chucked both cards out.

Three days' search of their local rubbish tip – with special permission from the council – failed to produce the cards and cost them the chance of scoring £100,000. The Wellingtons could only stare bleakly as all the rubbish was finally bulldozed into the ground.

'It was heartbreaking,' said Mrs Wellington. 'I tremble when I think how I put those cards into a rubbish bag.'

Matters were even worse for her husband John. His colleagues at work couldn't understand how a financial manager could have thrown away the chance of making a fortune.

Long-distance loving

Terry Jasper was pleased that his shy son had finally found the right girl. He thought it a little odd, however, that Damon, 19, never brought the girl home, although they chatted happily on the 'phone.

Girlfriend Donna had a very good reason for not popping round to the Jasper family home – she lived in Hong Kong. And the distance seemed even greater when Terry got the 'phone bill. Naturally, in view of the big part played by the telephone in Damon's romance, the lad's main wish was to get 'engaged'.

'When Donna's dad took her to Hong Kong that was bad enough but now my love life has turned into a terrible nightmare,' Damon complained. His father had ordered him to use the money he was saving for their wedding to pay for the 'phone calls.

Chapter Four

A FOOL AND HIS MONEY

Tales of some of the wealthiest people in the world being parted from their money – or at least some of it – make interesting reading. Are the rich really so gullible, or does greed make them temporarily blind?

Confidence tricks, frauds and hair-brained schemes to make money abound in these pages, along with one scheme that sounded daft but actually succeeded for the Canadian inventors of the hugely popular board game, Trivial Pursuit.

Oil's well that ends well . . .?

Count Alain de Villegas certainly impressed the directors of Elf, the French national oil company. This bizarre, but obviously brilliant Belgian seemed the answer to all France's problems. He had, he said, a remarkable solution to the country's oil shortage. With his colleague, an Italian scientist called Bonassoli, he had invented a machine so technically sophisticated that it could literally sniff out oil!

Because the Count had been introduced to them by Antoine Pinay, their country's former Prime Minister, the Elf executives had no reason to doubt his word. They conferred at a hush-hush meeting and decided that no less a person than President Giscard d'Estaing should be told of the discovery. The President, in turn, agreed that the project was so crucial to France's future that any money paid for the invention should come from special government funds.

The Count was duly handed a staggering 30 million pounds' worth of government money and set about building his magical black box. But the black box was such a sensitive secret, no one but he or Bonassoli were to be allowed to open it.

It was indeed an amazing piece of equipment. As reconnaissance planes flew over France's potential oil sites, the black box spewed out sharply defined maps showing where hidden oil deposits could be found.

The directors of Elf were ecstatic, and oil workers immediately began drilling umpteen bore-holes, expecting oil to gush forth at any moment.

But it was nothing like the 'digging for victory' they had anticipated. All the holes were bone dry. Not a single drop of oil was to be found.

Suspicions were aroused and, finally, the magic black box was forced open. Inside, all that was found was a set of maps . . . and a photocopier!

The French police immediately left for Belgium to apprehend the slippery con-man. But he proved as elusive as the supposed oil deposits – and was never seen again.

The gullible rich and towering deceits

It was back in the 1920s that the notorious 'Count' Victor Lustig and Daniel Collins 'sold' the Eiffel Tower. In fact, they had actually 'sold' it *twice* – to two separate scrap merchants. You would think no one would make the same mistake again; yet there was at least one man – a wealthy Texan – who had never heard the story.

Just after the Second World War, a con-man named Stanley Lowe offered the Eiffel Tower as scrap to the unsuspecting Texan. The Texan was on a visit to Paris when Lowe managed to convince him that the tower – one of the most famous monuments in the world – had been so badly damaged during the war that the city's officials had decided to sell it off as scrap. According to Lowe, the historic monument was up for sale at its scrap value – 25,000 dollars. The Texan bought the story lock, stock and barrel.

Luckily for the Texan – and for Paris – Lowe's con was discovered and he was sentenced to nine months in jail – an experience not entirely unknown to him. In fact, until his 'retirement', at the age of 50, he spent more than 16 years in prison for a variety of audacious frauds and cons. One was a spending spree in America, where he spent no less than 3,000 dollars of phony currency, crafted by a London counterfeiter named 'Johnny the Mask'. For that little jaunt, Lowe was deported.

Then there was the time he persuaded a Japanese tourist to part with 10,000 dollars to help restore London's St Paul's Cathedral. He had donned one of his large collection of clerical gowns for the occasion, just to add a bit of authenticity to the appeal.

Lowe fancied himself as a bit of a Robin Hood. 'I wanted to rob the rich,' he said. He claimed he simply couldn't help himself; people everywhere, it seemed, wanted to give him their money. And it could be so much fun, too. One day he would be Oscar-winning Hollywood producer Mark Sheridan, seeking investors for a new, guaranteed box-office smash; another day, he would become Group Captain Rivers Bogle-Bland and, despite the rather dubious double-barrelled tag, managed to convince people he was a war-time flying hero currently working undercover for the government on a secret mission.

The Eiffel Tower, sold to the man in the big hat at a knock-down price.

Lowe did not just extort from ordinary people; he would sometimes set his sights far higher – even as high as the Royal Family. Once, he smooth-talked his way into a job as a footman at Marlborough House, home of the late Queen Mary. Here, his plan was to steal as much as he could lay his hands on. But his taste for high living eventually betrayed him, when he arrived for work one day wearing a designer suit and driving a brand new Jaguar (which he had stolen) – a bit suspicious for a footman on £6 a week. When he was questioned by police, he explained, 'She (Queen Mary) is surrounded by priceless possessions, and I had nothing . . . It's not that I'm disloyal to our beloved Royal Family. I just decided she should be punished for her greed.'

Lowe, who had begun his life in an orphanage in north London and had developed into a small-time criminal, had the gift of the gab and was used to coping with tricky situations. Once, the owner of a Mayfair apartment caught him stealing. Cool, calm and collected, the con-man explained: 'Madam, this is an emergency. I was just passing when I saw a man attempting to hurl himself from the window.' Then, with his pockets full of jewellery, he swept past the astonished woman and was gone.

Stanley Lowe eventually ended his life living in a bed-sit. Gone were the days of hand-made shirts and shoes, the times when life revolved around magnums of champagne, weekends at the ritzy George V Hotel in Paris and luxury holidays in Bermuda – all paid for by clever cons involving the rich and gullible.

Under the hammer

Butcher Arthur Dawson thought he'd got a good price for the rusty old banger which had stood in his garage in Walsall for 30 years. He had sold it for £150,000 to a kindly car dealer – who didn't seem to mind about the bodywork falling apart and mice attacking the leather upholstery.

In fact, the 'rusty old banger' turned out to be a 1936 Mercedes–Benz tourer – a classic model of which just ten were made and only four still exist. And the 'kindly car dealer' had been John Price, who put his new purchase up for auction -- where it went for £1½ million.

The new, proud owner, millionaire Swedish property developer Hans Thulin, had spent the last 10 years scouring the world for the 500k Mercedes–Benz Special Roadster. 'I'll restore it and very soon it will be worth £5 million,' he said. 'But I'll never, ever sell it.'

All Mr Dawson could say was: 'I didn't do a very good deal, did I?'

Laughing all the way to the bank?

Chris Sandland, company secretary of Young's Brewery in Wandsworth, London, couldn't believe his eyes when he saw the latest bank statement showing that his company was £5 million in the black. 'We normally run with an overdraft of £2 million by the end of the year, so when the cashier mentioned the figure we didn't take too much notice – until we realized we were in credit.'

But Sandland's joy did not last for long. Five days later, he received a letter from a rather embarrassed customer services manager, Chris Green of the National Westminster Bank . . . asking for it all back! 'I was concerned,' Green had written, 'to learn that we have credited your account with the sum of 'five million pounds and no pence' in error. I can confirm that the necessary adjustment has been made to take the money back again.'

The bank had every reason to be embarrassed. Had they not picked up the error, in just those five days they stood to lose over £7,000 in interest payments!

Never trust a weatherman

Nearly two billion pounds was wiped off share values in February 1988, when reports of another Chernobyl nuclear disaster were flashed around the world.

The London stockmarket plunged, as dealers went wild at the news of a damaged Russian atomic plant spewing radioactive fallout all over Europe; America's White House was bombarded with frantic calls; the Swedes launched a fall-out alert along their border with Russia; while the Kremlin added to the chaos by refusing to deny or confirm the report.

Then red-faced weathermen in Britain had to admit it was all a false alarm. Staff at the Meteorological Centre in Bracknell, Berkshire, had dreamed up a bogus message to test the hotline to the International Atomic Energy Agency in Vienna. Somehow the message had appeared on a Telex machine and, suddenly, all hell had broken loose.

Said a Met Office spokesman: 'We can't figure out why the Telex message should suddenly appear and give people the fright of their lives.'

The big winner was the American dollar – it soared in two hours of frenzied trading.

Engineer turns property tycoon

Blundering engineer Bill Savin had gone along to a property auction in Bristol purely out of interest. He had just sold his own house and was curious to know what his money would buy. He came away the reluctant owner of a row of ten Regency houses worth £1.8 million!

Blundering Bill had raised his hand to scratch his nose, and before he had time to realize what had happened, his 'bid' had been accepted.

Bill was too embarrassed to tell the packed auction hall that he didn't want the prestige properties, or that he had nowhere near the money to pay for them. His confession came later, as the vendor's solicitors awaited their cheque for £1,800,000.

Bill finally got his own solicitor, Richard Castle, to get him out of the mess. Said Castle: 'Mr Savin is just an ordinary chap who does not have the money for such a property deal. It was just a terrible error. The vendor's solicitors seem to understand it was just a ghastly mistake.' Later, another auction was called to sell the houses, this time to a *bona fide* developer.

I am a camera – fly me!

It seemed like a great idea at the time – you bought a camera and got a cut-price flight. The promotional scheme, hatched by TWA and Polaroid in the United States, would sell cameras *and* fill airline seats. The customers would be getting a bargain, too. Yet the scheme went down as one of the biggest boobs in the history of sales stunts.

What the high-flying executives at TWA and Polaroid forgot to do was to add to the small print: 'Only one camera per person.' The result was that, for the price of a 20-dollar camera, snap-happy Americans could buy a cut-price airline ticket to anywhere they fancied. The more cameras they bought, the more tickets they could buy and the more money they saved.

Soon, travel agents were buying cameras by the thousand, giving customers huge discounts over and over again. Shrewd businessmen made fortunes by scooping up caseloads of cameras and selling the discount vouchers to companies with large travel bills: the McDonnell-Douglas Corporation bought 1000 coupons at 10 dollars each, and saved 200,000 dollars on their executives' travel expenses.

While Polaroid chiefs celebrated their massive boom in camera sales, TWA executives admitted ruefully: 'We left some big loopholes.'

Der Führer's secret life

A ny newspaper in the world would have been happy to pay a fortune for the ultimate scoop: the private, unpublished diaries of Adolf Hitler, spanning a watershed in world history, from 1932 to 1945.

The German news magazine *Stern* could not afford to miss the chance of boosting its circulation sky-high – for an outlay of £2.5 million. This was the sum paid for exclusive world rights to the Nazi leader's intimate, day to day revelations. And for becoming the victim of what has been called the literary hoax of the century.

The 'Hitler Diaries', touted to the world as the scoop of all time, were all fake, the work of a con-man who became obsessed with his forgery and fooled hardbitten newspaper executives and historical experts.

It was in 1983 that *Stern*, and that most reputable British newspaper, *The Sunday Times*, announced the existence of volumes of Der Führer's wartime jottings. No one had any reason to suspect that their publication was the

Heidemann shows the books *Stern* claims are Adolf Hitler's diaries.

result of collaboration and collusion between two men, one of whom was a 53-year-old award winning journalist, Gerd Heidemann, who worked for *Stern*, the magazine he was to defraud.

The other was a small time forger, Konrad Kujau, 46, who had been running a profitable sideline in counterfeit luncheon vouchers. He was, in fact, a talented artist with a fertile imagination and a feeling for fantasy.

Kujau supplemented his living by selling antiques, especially war memorabilia. He never missed a chance to pull a fast one on eager collectors, cashing in on their cravings for material, and was not above manufacturing his own certificates of authenticity. He 'aged' the documents by soaking them in tea – a technique that was to earn him a fortune from news-hungry editors throughout the world.

Then he moved on to paintings, supposedly done by Hitler. This line was to lead to his relationship with another keen collector of Nazi memorabilia, Fritz Stiefel, which sparked off the Hitler diary hoax.

Stiefel often bought items for his collection from Kujau, who decided, in return for his faithful custom, to treat him to a real gem, a diary written in the Führer's own fair hand.

News of the startling find soon reached the ears of *Stern* journalist Gerd Heidemann, who was also obsessed with the Third Reich.

Heidemann never doubted the authenticity of the new discovery. As any experienced reporter would do, he embarked on background research and learnt, to his great excitement, that a courier aircraft had crashed near the Czechoslovakian border towards the end of the Second World War. The plane, flying from Berlin, had carried secret papers belonging to Hitler. There was every reason to suppose that the diaries had been among them.

Stern, when it published the astonishing diaries scoop, added that Heidemann had managed to obtain the historic material from 'East German contacts'. The papers had been discovered in a hay loft where they had supposedly been hidden after the plane crash.

Heidemann could scarcely wait to tell his superiors about his find, but senior editors Peter Koch and Felix Schmidt dismissed his scoop as yet another piece of obsessive fabrication.

It was Thomas Walde, a senior *Stern* journalist, who unwittingly became part of the hoax. He and Heidemann together succeeded in convincing *Stern*'s top management that they should offer Kujau two million German marks for the priceless diaries. Walde and Heidemann were assigned to follow up the story.

Kujau was beside himself with joy. He couldn't believe his luck, and set about his work with relish. If *Stern* wanted Hitler's war diaries, they would have them – as many as they wished. Such was Kujau's enthusiasm for the project that he compiled a prodigious output of 62 faked volumes.

It seems incredible now that *Stern* and a host of eminent academics could have been taken in by some of the entries.

'Friday, 13th: Ten thousand communists meet in Berlin Sports Palace, pledge will fight fascism to last breath. Demonstration, many arrests. By Jove, we must stamp out the Reds.

Saturday, 14th: Meet all the leaders of the storm troopers in Bavaria, give them medals. They pledge lifelong loyalty to the Führer, with tears in their eyes. What a splendid body of men!'

Kujau claimed smugly that 'Hitler's life' had taken him no time at all to record. As the money kept on coming, he had simply kept on writing, and with each fake entry his confidence grew.

Of the famous bomb plot against Hitler by the German Generals, Kujau recorded gleefully: 'Ha! Ha! Isn't it laughable? These people were bunglers. This scum, these loafers and good-for-nothings!'

The Sunday Times had in all good faith bought the rights and had started to publish extracts when the scandal broke. A correspondent, Frank Johnson, wrote in *The Times* in March 1985: 'At least when *The Sunday Times* published its first extract, your present correspondent, a lifelong amateur student of mid-20th-century European politics, had no doubt that the diaries were genuine; they were so boring.

Hitler exerts his fascination with his deeds rather than his prose. On that Sunday, those of us familiar with *Mein Kampf*, *The Collected Speeches* and *Table Talk* knew that this was the authentic voice.'

Kujau and Heidemann were arrested in May 1983 for faking up the world scoop. Heidemann, his record as a star writer ruined for ever, was charged with defrauding the magazine of £2.5 million, paid in instalments between January 1981 and April 1983. He maintained throughout the 11-month trial in Hamburg that he had believed the diaries to be genuine.

Kujau was charged with forgery which had earned him £415,000. He admitted guilt. Indeed, he basked in the attention he attracted during the court proceedings.

The prosecution's case against the forgers filled 4,000 pages and involved 62 witnesses and eight experts. Eminent historian Lord Dacre of Glanton, who had at first declared the diaries to be genuine, had the courage to admit his mistake. He attended a conference called by *Stern* in Hamburg in April 1983, where he expressed his doubts about the value of the scoop and he tried to warn *The Sunday Times* about the risks.

As the trial dragged on, fascinating evidence was heard, producing copy as riveting to readers as the fake scoop.

A Professor Eberhard Jaeckel had published some of Kujau's 'war documents' before the big scandal broke. Experts had seen through them straight away.

A *Sunday Times* reporter, Gita Sereny, had been dispatched to Germany after a tip-off about the diaries, but she had not been allowed to visit Jaeckel because of the extra cost it would have involved.

Stern executives had given a page of the 'diaries' to experts to study, without explaining why. The experts they had engaged did not know what they were looking for and passed the copies as authentic.

The ink and tea-soaked paper used for the diaries had not been tested until it was too late.

Kujau said he at first intended to write only three diaries in return for a uniform worn by Hermann Göring and which Heidemann had shown him.

'I had to have it,' he told the court. He had forged one Hitler diary in 1978 because it annoyed him that the Führer had apparently left no records of his life. Kujau said he was sure Heidemann had tumbled his trickery after he wrote the word 'helmet' in Hitler's script on a piece of paper which the reporter saw.

To prove the *Stern* reporter's obsession with Hitler, German police raided his home. They took photographs of objects which had once adorned Hitler's desk, including a swastika on a red background which Heidemann said was Hitler's 'martyr's flag'. Heidemann also had in his bizarre collection a pair of underpants that had once belonged to Idi Amin.

Heidemann told the court that Kujau had also offered him an unpublished volume of Hitler's autobiography *Mein Kampf*. 'When I heard the diaries were fakes, I wondered whether to shoot myself then or later,' Heidemann said.

Kujau claimed Heidemann had first told him he wanted the diaries so that they could be sent to Martin Bormann, Hitler's former deputy in South America. 'Heidemann said the diaries would help to rehabilitate Bormann but I began to doubt the story. Then in January 1982, Heidemann told me Bormann was seriously ill and I should hurry my work.'

Heidemann and Kujau's con was rumbled when experts at the Federal Archives in Koblenz were finally allowed to examine some of the writings. They declared them 'primitive fakes' on postwar paper.

Kujau had apparently outsmarted himself. Although he'd checked facts and dates about Hitler before creating the diaries, he did not realize, when he bought the Gothic letters in Hong Kong to stick on the diary covers, that he had mixed up the letters A and F. The imitation metal initials 'FH' instead of 'AH' adorned the volumes.

The court couldn't help but snigger when it heard that Kujau had once provided the obsessed Heidemann with fake ashes of Hitler, supplied by a friend who worked in a crematorium.

Heidemann and Kujau were both found guilty on 8 July, 1985. Heidemann was jailed for four years and eight months and Kujau for four years and six months.

Kujau's girlfriend, Edith Lieblang, had also been involved. She was accused of spending part of the ill-gotten gains and was given an eight-month suspended sentence. No one found out where all the money went.

Poor Thomas Walde was grilled in court for his gullibility.

The whole world knew the Hitler diaries were a fake.

Heidemann's friends said he had been used as a scapegoat by *Stern*, whose weekly circulation dropped by 100,000 when the deception was announced.

The Sunday Times had already agreed to pay £250,000 for the extracts. Too late, Lord Dacre realized his first assessment was wrong. In *The Times* of May 19, 1983, he admitted making 'a grave error' and claimed he had been misled by *Stern*.

Stern editors Peter Koch and Felix Schmidt were fired even though they had been kept in the dark about the diary dealings.

Gerd Schulte-Hillen, managing director of *Stern* owners Grüner and Jahr, had inherited the diaries from his predecessor Henri Nannen but had backed Heidemann, refusing to believe that he was involved in a major fraud. He was allowed to stay on at *Stern*.

Frank Giles, editor of *The Sunday Times*, retired to become 'editor emeritus'. In *Selling Hitler, the Story of the Hitler Diaries*, author Richard Harris tells how Rupert Murdoch, owner of *The Sunday Times*, justified Giles's new title. 'It's Latin. The 'e' means you're out and 'meritus' means you deserve it.'

Continues Harris: 'Murdoch, who ordered *The Sunday Times* to continue printing even when he had been told that Lord Dacre was sounding the alarm, commented: 'After all, we're in the entertainment business.'

All that glitters

To the aristocrats assembled in a Munich hotel, it seemed the golden opportunity they had been waiting for – a conspiracy of silence which was sure to make their fortune. All eyes were upon the stranger who had invited them to witness his amazing demonstration that night.

Hans Unruh spoke intently: 'I must ask you to treat what I am about to tell you with the strictest confidence. This is not a secret to be shared, but one we must keep strictly to ourselves. It is very important. And it could be dangerous.'

He picked up a salt cellar and brandished it before his captivated audience. He explained that the cellar contained a rare and very precious commodity. Gold.

Some guests sniggered, others sat in silent disbelief. But they all listened as Unruh continued.

He was a scientist, he went on. And he had discovered how gold was made. It came from the depths of the earth where it was created by a chemical action on ordinary salt. If some method could be discovered of reproducing this chemical change artificially, unlimited quantities of gold could be manufactured from the world's salt supplies.

He showed his enthralled audience a simple piece of apparatus – a green lampshade. Research had proved that if you treated salt with a special form of light it would turn into pure gold, he told them.

Unruh knew the good and wealthy people he was addressing would need proof of this miracle. He took hold of the salt cellar and gently tapped some of the salt on to a steel plate. Then he took the lamp and held it in such a way that the shade completely covered the dish.

He switched the lamp on and waited a few moments. When he finally removed the shade, the onlookers were speechless. There on the plate, where grains of salt had lain, bright flecks of gold dust were glittering. To emphasize the value of the little pile, Unruh scooped it up and tipped it into a small bag.

By now, disbelief had turned into avid interest. Unruh had his guests under his spell. This was the moment to explain that he was a struggling scientist and that his discovery had to be exploited to the full. Money would be needed to provide equipment for the large-scale manufacture of gold. 'You are wealthy, of proven integrity and have a great sense of responsibility. You have all been specially selected for this opportunity,' Unruh told his guests. 'I wish you to all become shareholders in my enterprise. Perhaps you would like to go away and think it over.'

Already, guests were inquiring how much the shares would cost. Little did they know it was Unruh, and not his gullible guests, who had struck gold. He made £3,500 from the evening's show, thanks to a simple trick which had completely fooled the sons and daughters of Germany's finest families. The 'gold dust' had been concealed in the green lampshade, and when Unruh tapped it, it showered down, covering the salt. Closer inspection would have given him away, because brass, with the light shining on it, looks just like gold.

Too trivial for words

Ray Loud and Steve Birch had to laugh when two quirky Canadians with whom they had been drinking sangria on holiday in Spain in 1974 tried to involve them in a hare-brained scheme to make an easy fortune.

The enterprising Canadians, Chris Haney and Scott Abbott, had invented a board game they were convinced was going to make them rich, and they wanted Ray and Steve to help them by writing down a lot of daft questions while the dice were thrown.

'We were playing this silly game on the back of a table mat at a barbecue in Spain,' Ray recalled. 'It was good fun but nothing more – or so we thought. We just burst out laughing when Chris and Scott asked us to be the writers of the British version of their game. We didn't want to be caught up in a crazy scheme.'

They might have changed their minds if they had known that they had just turned down a chance to share in the success of the world's biggest board game blockbuster of all time – Trivial Pursuit.

Less than ten years after its creation, the game was being played in four million British homes and in 50 million homes throughout the world. Trivial Pursuit earned Scott, Chris, and his brother John Haney £25 million and established a cult following from Hollywood to the White House. There was a 10-day Trivial Pursuit cruise on *QE2*; 78 editions went on sale in 17 different languages; and addicts in 31 countries, including Iceland and Japan, couldn't stop playing it. At the height of Trivial Pursuit mania, four students in Doncaster, Yorkshire, claimed an entry in *The Guinness Book of Records* for playing non-stop for five days.

The success story began when Scott and Chris sat idly over their beers one day, marvelling at the amount of money Scrabble must have made for its creators. Within 45 minutes they had come up with the basis for their own money-spinner.

'We wanted the game to be a kind of party in a box, with lots of fun for all ages and types, and we figured if we creased up laughing, others would too,' Chris said. 'To test our game, we dragged people off the street, gave them a glass of wine, and bombarded them with silly questions.'

The game ended happily for its clever creators, who were able to live in luxury, thanks to their bright idea.

The Trivial Pursuit that brought tremendous rewards.

Ray Loud and Steve Birch did not miss out after all. They were given a second opportunity to cash in, two years after the first approach. This time they jumped at the chance to write the questions for the British version, and went on to reap the rewards.

Goose down

This was one goose which would never lay a golden egg, not even for its creator, the fabulously wealthy Howard Hughes. To the billionaire, ploughing £18 million into a giant wooden flying boat, the *Spruce Goose*, seemed a good idea at the time. The eight-engined seaplane, commissioned in 1942 and designed to hold 700 troops, wasn't finished until the end of the war.

Hughes hit the heights at the controls of the *Spruce Goose* on 2 November 1947, in a maiden – the one-and-only – flight, which lasted for just one minute, over the waters of Long Beach Harbor. The *Spruce Goose* reached a height of 70 feet, then took a dive, never to see the light of day again.

It remained in a hangar in California gathering dust for 33 years. In 1980, four years after the death of the rich recluse, the city of Long Beach wanted the machine taken out of the hangar, so that the hangar could be used as an oil terminal.

The *Spruce Goose* was dismantled in such a way that nine museums throughout America could each have a part of the aircraft to display. 'The decision to do this was an emotional one for all of us involved,' said Fred Lewis, a spokesman for the Summa Corporation of America.

The goose that took a dive and its creator, Howard Hughes.

Prince – or pauper

The film star always had her eyes open for a man – preferably famous or rich – who would woo her. And she thought her ship had come in when a young man sought out her company during a holiday in Monte Carlo. For she'd heard him being paged – the call went out for Prince Urbano of Barberini. The two engaged in conversation and for several days the film star and the Prince were inseparable.

A yet deeper impression was made when he dropped the names of the local royal family into conversation.

Trying to do the right thing, the film star picked up the bills on a trip to Paris. She did not want to be seen as a gold digger. And they went Dutch when dining at exclusive restaurants. Only later did she discover the teenage Romeo was just an ordinary lad who'd always wanted to meet her.

Chapter Five

CATASTROPHES

The 1980s will be remembered as a decade with more than its share of tragedy. Who can forget the horror of the Zeebrugge disaster, in which 193 people perished as the Townsend Thoresen ferry capsized, the American Independence Day error which cost nearly 300 innocent people on board an Iranian passenger plane their lives, or the death of teacher Christa McAuliffe and her six fellow astronauts in the ill-fated Challenger?

   These quite recent happenings and the stories of catastrophes from earlier days lament the fate of the innocent victims of aggression and human error.

87

Zeebrugge

The trip to the Continent had been a fun day, the ferry passengers agreed. Now they were safely on board for the return crossing to Dover, with time to relax on board as the late winter's evening closed in.

Some of the 436 passengers stood on deck to watch the quay at the Belgian port of Zeebrugge receding as they sailed home; others gathered at the bar. Children scampered about, over-tired and excited, while their parents put their feet up in the lounges or prepared to enjoy a cup of tea in the restaurant of the 7,951 ton Townsend Thoresen ferry, *Herald of Free Enterprise*.

The ferry's 60 crew members made preparations to sail and to do brisk business in the bars and the duty free shop. David Lewry, the ship's captain, had made the trip many times before, and just after 6 pm his vessel was under way, with its passengers, 36 lorries and 84 cars all secure.

Moments later, the happy holiday ship turned into an icy tomb for hundreds of innocent men, women and children as the ferry capsized and the dark North Sea flooded in.

Many died instantly in the first minutes of horror. Screaming passengers were sucked out of smashed windows, others were crushed as furniture and fittings caved in, vehicles were hurled over the capsized ferry and people fought for their lives in a nightmare of rising sea water.

That night, 6 March, 1987, 193 people perished in what a survivor described as a scene from hell.

One passenger told his own story of the tragedy. He had been sitting in the top bar with a friend when they felt the boat keel over without warning. They sat for a moment, stunned. 'As she went, one of the windows nearest the waterline broke and people were pulled out of the window. We grabbed hold of the seats nearest to us and just held on to them.

'The ferry turned right over on her side and my friend and I were thrown into the water. He managed to get back and we scrambled on to the seats, just moving up with the water level until it seemed to have stopped rising.

'I got hold of one child who was passed to us to keep it above water level. Those who were able to do so climbed the tables and chairs to get out of the broken window and some were pulled up with ropes, hosepipes, anything they could get hold of.

The capsized *Herald of Free Enterprise* outside Zeebrugge.

'Finally, the rescue boats and helicopters arrived. The rescuers broke the windows. It seemed like an eternity but it was probably only 10 to 15 minutes before they came on the scene.'

Many of the passengers were taken to hospital at nearby Knokke. The ship's cook, Paul White, was one of them.

'I've been on that run for 14 years,' he said, 'but I can't understand what happened. It just went over. People started to scream. Some had put on life jackets in the darkness. It was the only thing they could see because of the fluorescent strips.'

Many passengers tumbled straight into the icy sea, 30 feet deep at that point. The ferry had only just passed out of the harbour entrance when disaster struck.

A 16-minute replay evokes the tragedy.

6.10 pm: Everyone aboard. The ship, which can accommodate 1,000 passengers, is less than half full.

6.11 pm: The *Herald of Free Enterprise* heads for home.

6.15 pm: Some lorry drivers and motorists make a last check to see if their vehicles are secure on the roll on-roll off vessel.

6.22 pm: The crew hear a strange coded message from the captain. The passengers are unaware of the emergency call.

6.25 pm: The ferry starts to list, and with a violent lurch is thrust on its side.

6.26 pm: Terror reigns as the North Sea grips the sinking ship.

A massive rescue operation was launched within minutes. Even though the *Herald* had only left the harbour, it was to take many exhausting, heroic hours before rescue operations were completed. Helpers were still racing against a rising morning tide the next day to find those still missing and to lift off the dead.

The floodlit scene after the disaster was sinister as the tug *Fighter* from Antwerp and its two sister vessels, working in adverse conditions, moved in to help. Helicopter searchlights cast an eerie, blitz–like glow over the scene of death.

Belgian and Dutch authorities had acted swiftly. Navy helicopters rushed to the scene. Experts from a Dutch salvage firm sent vessels and divers to Zeebrugge. Britain joined in the rescue effort as soon as it heard of the tragic plight of its people. Two RAF Sea King helicopters with divers were sent from the Culdrose Royal Navy base in Cornwall. The destroyer HMS *Glasgow* and frigate HMS *Diomede* joined the rescue teams. An RAF Nimrod aircraft with life saving equipment was on emergency stand-by.

While some of the ferry's passengers still fought for their lives, others were taken to hospital. Bodies, too many to count in the dark chaos, lay battered in the watery grave.

A hasty message, chalked up at Townsend Thoresen's embarkation point in the Zeebrugge terminal, stated bleakly: 'Due to an incident in the port, all sailings are temporarily suspended. You will be notified as soon as sailings are resumed.'

Many passengers waiting for the next ferry to Dover that night remained standing on the dockside, unsure why they were not allowed to embark. Their children tugged at their sleeves, too young to understand that a terrible tragedy was happening at sea.

Four men, including Captain David Lewry, were singled out for making the fatal mistakes that turned the 132-metre ferry into a watery tomb.

Mr Justice Sheen, chairman of the Zeebrugge inquiry in July 1987, stated the cause of the disaster clearly: 'The *Herald* sank because she went to sea with her inner and outer bow doors open.'

The assistant bosun, Marc Stanley, who was responsible for closing the bow doors before the ship sailed, had been fast asleep at the time. He awoke when he was thrown from his bunk as the crippled ferry turned on her side. Chief Officer Leslie Sabel was accused of being 'seriously negligent' for not checking that the doors were closed before sailing. The *Herald*'s senior master, Captain John Kirby, was told he must 'bear the responsibility for the disaster' for not issuing clear orders about closing the doors. And the inquiry found that Captain Lewry had also been seriously negligent in taking his ship to sea in an 'unsafe condition'.

Mr Justice Sheen, who had sat with four assessors for 29 days, ordered the immediate suspension of Captain Lewry's master's certificate for a year and Chief Officer Leslie Sabel's certificate for two years.

It had seemed at first, said the judge, that responsibility rested with the *Herald*'s captain and crew. But on reflection, blame lay higher up in Townsend Thoresen's management where 'cardinal faults' came to light. Mr Justice Sheen said the board of directors had not appreciated their responsibility for safety on their ships and that the directors lacked a proper understanding of their duties.

'From top to bottom, the body was infected by the disease of sloppiness,' was his indictment.

He criticized standing orders issued to the *Herald* by management for not including express instructions to close the bow and storm doors. This had led the captain to believe erroneously that the ship was ready to sail.

The inquiry noted that the ship's masters had in the past, in internal memos, expressed concern to management about safety. This had fallen on deaf ears ashore. The *Herald* was not the first of the company's ferries to sail with its cargo door open. This had happened on several other occasions, and these incidents had led one of the masters, two years previously, to suggest that indicator lights were needed on the bridge to show whether or not the doors had been shut.

The inquiry considered that if this had received 'the serious consideration it deserved', it was at least possible that the lights would have been fitted in the early months of 1986 and disaster prevented.

After a month-long inquest, it took a jury in Dover nine hours to reach verdicts of unlawful killing of the 192 victims who died that cold, bitter night. Another passenger had died some time later in hospital, bringing the death toll to 193.

The British Government called for changes at the International Maritime Organisation (IMO) to ensure that members' ships would have door indicator lights, TV monitoring of the vehicle deck and back-up emergency lighting. Following the inquest verdict, Britain's Department of Public Prosecutions prepared charges against Townsend Thoresen, to make sure a similar British sea catastrophe would not occur.

CATASTROPHES

The heroes

Queen Elizabeth honoured 27 heroes of the Zeebrugge tragedy with personal thanks and medals for their bravery. They included Lieutenant Guido Couwenbergh of the Belgian Navy, a brave frogman who had singlehandedly saved the lives of 40 drowning people.

He was the first person to plunge into the icy sea and make his way to the sinking ferry's main café area where most of the victims were trapped. He received the Queen's Gallantry Medal.

At the Buckingham Palace ceremony he said: 'I thank God I managed to save so many but I can never forget the poor people who drifted away from me into the darkness to die.'

Andrew Parker, a Londoner, received the George Medal, Britain's second highest peacetime bravery award. He had helped save more than 120 fellow passengers by allowing them to use him as a human ladder to climb to safety.

The Queen honoured Belgian civilian diver Piet Lagast for saving the life of 15-year-old Nicola Simpson from Welwyn Garden City, Hertfordshire. Lagast received the Queen's Gallantry Medal after the monarch heard how he had rescued Nicola and eight others trapped behind a glass screen by shattering it with his diver's knife and cutting his hand to the bone in the process.

Nicola had suffered a heart attack as her body temperature dropped 25 degrees below normal. She became known as the 'Ice Maiden' after surviving four hours in the freezing waters. She was in fact certified dead on arrival at a Belgian hospital and declared clinically dead several times after her ordeal, but made an amazing recovery, only to learn that her mother had died in the tragedy.

The leader of the 40-strong Belgian Navy diving team, Lieutenant-Commander Alfons Daems, was also honoured for rescue work. 'There can be no joy here after being involved in such a major tragedy,' was his poignant response.

The hapless

The 42 crew members who survived were still suffering serious mental anguish a year later. Only two returned to sea, trying to forget their 38 dead colleagues.

The surviving crew underwent intense counselling to encourage them to talk about the horror of hearing their trapped friends screaming pitifully for help. Marriages foundered as men underwent personality changes in the aftermath of the sinking.

Children, especially, found it hard to forget what they had suffered. One little boy had recurrent dreams that his world had turned upside down and people were flying into the air.

One ferry hero, Londoner Colin Baines, was jailed for two and a half years after turning to drug dealing in the wake of the Zeebrugge tragedy. He had lost his brother-in-law and niece and was injured trying to save passengers from the stricken vessel. He had needed psychiatric help after the horror.

Baines was arrested after trying to sell £34,000 worth of cannabis, found in a bag belonging to his brother-in-law.

The horror

The Zeebrugge horror was re-enacted 18 months later when British and French rescue services created a similar tragedy to test contingency plans in the event of another shipping disaster.

The dark night was relived again at a memorial service 12 months after the ferry went down. Wreaths of flowers were lovingly tossed on to the waters off the Belgian coast by the grieving.

One touching card attached to a tribute read: 'Daddy – miss you.'

Those who could not bear to return to the scene that reminded them of lost loved ones attended a service at St Mary's Church, Dover, where a stained-glass window in memory of the dead was unveiled. Nearly 2,000 seamen marched in silence through Dover to the church.

The *Herald*'s captain continued to be haunted by the tragedy. 'I have been over it again and again so many times,' Captain Lewry recalled bitterly.

'I blacked out when it was happening but most of it stays with me. I wished I was dead. Sometimes I still do.'

His ship, the *Herald of Free Enterprise*, died a shameful death. A year after the disaster, the rusting vessel, renamed *Flushing Range*, was towed to rest in a Taiwanese breakers' yard.

All's unfair in love and war

The bitter fight between Iran and Iraq was at first called 'the whirlwind war' but after eight years the fighting was still fierce.

The battle that became the Gulf War started in 1980 when the Iraqi army sent its tanks across the international frontier from Basra into Iran. Iraqi soldiers believed they would be singing victoriously a few weeks later.

When they captured the bridge across the Karun River and that moment of glory ended in their blood-spattered bodies piling up in the dusty streets, the scene was set for a long-played-out conflict.

Vessels from Britain and America were called in to act as peace-keepers. Ironically, the mission earned Captain Will C. Rogers a tragic place in the history of the conflict. From his American warship, USS *Vincennes*, he gave an order to fire. Moments later, 290 innocent men, women and children were dead – in error. It was not an enemy fighter plane Captain Rogers's warship had blasted from the sky, but an Iranian jetliner on a scheduled domestic flight.

The tragedy happened on 4 July – Independence Day, traditionally a festive occasion for Americans. In 1988, it became a day of international outrage against their country.

The American cruiser detected Flight 655 to Dubai shortly after it took off from Bandar Abbas at 10.45 am. Captain Rogers and his US Navy crew had cause to feel threatened at the time. Earlier that morning a helicopter from the *Vincennes* had been fired on by Iranian fast attack craft.

A warning shot in the hostile atmosphere of the Gulf was not an unusual event, but tension was running particularly high that day. Western diplomats expected the Iranians to strike a blow against the Americans to coincide with the 4 July festivities, in order to focus public attention on their cause.

Captain Rogers was sure the attack on the *Vincennes* helicopter would lead to something more serious, and ordered his warship to retaliate, crippling two of the Iranian aircraft.

Five minutes after the Iranians' attack, the ill-fated A300 Airbus was picked up by the radar system on the *Vincennes*. It was later claimed that attempts were made to contact the Airbus on both military and civilian radio frequencies. The transponder on the Airbus should have identified the aircraft to the *Vincennes*. It was stated that at least six warnings were sent from the American warship, but no response, either friendly or hostile, came back.

Captain Rogers believed a US Navy ship was under threat by an F-14 fighter. At 10.51 am, the silent aircraft was declared the enemy. Three minutes later two standard ER2 missiles were fired at the target, destroying it at a range of six miles.

The 290 civilians who perished included 57 children aged between two and 12 years and nine babies. Passengers included not only Iranian but Indian, Pakistani, Italian, Afghan and Yugoslav nationals.

The Pentagon frantically issued statements to ward off international hostility. Officials said it had not been clear whether the plane was operating as a normal civilian airliner at the time of the shooting. The aircraft was flying well below commercial airspace and was broadcasting on a military frequency. It was descending upon the *Vincennes* when it was fired at, they claimed. Instead of climbing to the normal scheduled altitude above 20,000 feet it had levelled off at a dangerously low 9,000 feet.

The US Government was determined to portray the incident as a legitimate act of self defence 'when hostile intent was manifested', but some naval experts voiced their doubts. How could the highly sophisticated radar system on the *Vincennes* have failed to differentiate between friend and foe?

A less sophisticated source, the *ABC World Airways Guide*, widely used by travel agents, would have told those on board the *Vincennes* that the aircraft they were tracking had left within three minutes of the scheduled departure time of the fated Flight 655 to Dubai.

A former British anti-air-warfare officer later stated that any British warships in the Gulf would have records of civilian traffic patterns which would have been fed into a 'battle computer'.

A former US Navy officer said Iranian civilian aircraft had been challenged many times, but always gave the friendly response. No satisfactory explanation could be found for the fact that the Airbus was five miles outside the civilian air lane between Bandar Abbas and its destination of Dubai, or why the pilot allegedly ignored warnings.

It was suggested the Airbus might have been leading an Iranian fighter in its radar 'shadow' for an attack on the *Vincennes*.

Iran stated it would 'exploit to the utmost American barbarism as the innocent victim of the unprovoked massacre', but refrained from immediate retaliation.

No one will ever know the full story behind the Independence Day tragedy of 1988.

All hopes of piecing together those last few, fatal minutes must have sunk with the Airbus's flight recorder. Its recovery was never announced.

On 11 July, President Reagan announced America would offer compensation to the families of all 290 passengers. On 20 July, the Pentagon admitted errors were made by Captain Rogers and the crew of the *Vincennes*, but claimed the mistakes were not due to negligence. Defence Secretary Frank Carlucci said Captain Rogers had acted 'prudently on the basis of information available to him.'

No disciplinary action was taken against the warship's captain or any member of the crew.

Admiral William Crowe, chairman of the Joint Chiefs of Staff, said individual mistakes were not 'crucial' in the decision to attack the Iranian passenger plane.

'There was no culpable conduct displayed on board the *Vincennes*. This regrettable accident was a by-product of the Iran-Iraq war.'

But a senior Pentagon naval officer made his feelings clear. 'To hell with the Navy taking all the responsibility. Blame the politicians. They send us out there and tell us we can take anything in the sky which threatens us and then start raising questions when something goes wrong.'

Captain Rogers had made a poignant statement before sailing for the Middle East on the peace-keeping mission. 'If we are attacked or face hostile intent we will defend ourselves, but we are certainly not out there to create hostility.'

The 44-year-old Captain shouldered the deaths of nearly 300 innocent people on his own. 'I and I alone am responsible,' he said. 'This is a burden I will carry for the rest of my life.'

The *Vincennes* was relieved of duty in the Gulf later that year during a ceasefire between Iraq and Iran. American officials said the 96,000 ton warship was officially detached from the navy's Middle East joint task force. Shortly after the ceasefire was announced, machine guns opened fire on a Norwegian tanker in the Gulf . . . and the war continued, and with unjust, irrational actions.

Teaching from the sky

igh school teacher Christa McAuliffe could not contain her exuberance at the thought of the big step she was about to take for womankind. The 37-year-old mother of two had been picked from among 11,000 eager American applicants to make the epic space journey on board the US shuttle Challenger.

Dawn broke bitterly cold in Florida on 28 January, 1986, the day of the launch. Christa had kissed and hugged her children Scott, 9, and Caroline, 6, goodbye the night before. They were still sleeping but would soon, with their father Steve, and family and friends, witness at first hand the historic launch at Cape Canaveral. The McAuliffe children were the envy of all small girls and boys who have ever dreamt about becoming one of the elite band of American astronauts. The whole world was waiting with baited breath to see live televised broadcasts of Challenger blasting off into the blue.

Christa had enjoyed an early supper with her lawyer husband the night before and had kissed him goodbye at the crew quarters. It was not the happy occasion she would have wanted. With her six fellow astronauts Christa had had to accept with great disappointment the news that the launch had been postponed for 24 hours because of technical problems.

They had set off brightly past all the waiting newsmen who were waving and smiling. Then they all had to return to crew quarters to kick their heels as the freezing weather delayed the launch. The mission had already been postponed three times before.

Christa killed time by calling the teacher who was replacing her. She joked about how funny it was they were all due to be launched in a billion-dollar shuttle, and no one could find a tool box for last minute repairs.

Meanwhile, the temperature continued to plummet to sub-freezing. Arctic winds were blowing at the shuttle's proposed launch time of 9.38 am.

The launch-pad team grew increasingly worried about the ice forming around the shuttle. The temperature had dropped to 24° Fahrenheit, the wind chill to 10 below zero. The ground crew had kept the water running to prevent the pipes that fed the fire-extinguishing system from freezing.

Christa woke at 6.20 am on the day of the launch. She showered, pulled on her blue jeans and sneakers and joined the rest of the crew for a light

The Challenger lift-off.

breakfast. The cooks had prepared a special surprise for them – a white-frosted cake decorated with the Challenger's emblem and all their names. Christa's was there, together with shuttle pilot Michael Smith, Commander Francis Scobbe, Ronald McNair, Ellison Onizuka, Gregory Jarvis and female astronaut Judy Resnick.

At 7.20 am they received their final orders and a weather briefing. None knew just how bitterly cold it was . . . or how great a threat the freezing weather posed to their safety. A few moments later Commander Scobbe led the crew down the ramp past the roped-off throng of photographers. Christa's excitement mounted once more. This time they were off! Even the icicles, several feet long, hanging from the launch tower gave her no cause for concern. She was confident that nothing would go wrong and she laughed when someone in the crowd handed her a bright red apple, as red as her own cheeks in the freezing air. 'Save it for me and I'll eat it when I get back,' she shouted.

By this time Christa's husband and children, her sister, Betsy Corrigan, and her parents Grace and Ed Corrigan, were standing in a prime vantage area, waiting for the countdown and holding hands in their excitement.

They knew astronaut Judy Resnick would be the second woman in space, but their Christa was to be the first teacher in space.

The world was watching too and millions saw the expression on those faces, now shining with pride, later change to grief and horror, at what they saw. Betsy Corrigan screamed in despair and Steve hustled the children away in stunned silence after Christa and the rest of the Challenger crew were blown from the sky before their very eyes – turning the historic moment into tragedy.

The billion-dollar shuttle exploded at 1,977 miles an hour with the force of a small nuclear weapon one minute and 12 seconds after launch, shattering the lives of the crew and their close ones and destroying America's entire space programme in one almighty blast.

Christa and her space friends died in an explosion of 526,000 gallons of liquid hydrogen and liquid oxygen as the 90-ton shuttle shattered into thousands of pieces. At first the world was told they had all died instantly, but months later the full horror emerged. NASA's cameras and the American television networks recorded the disaster in terrifying detail.

Long after the original fireball that marked the explosion, a red-orange and white inferno that stunned spectators, came the smoking trails of debris etched across the clear wintry sky. So much debris was falling down that it was unsafe to send out search parties for nearly an hour. Frogmen later scoured the waters off the Florida coast, looking for bodies. They had been instructed to recover even the smallest fragments of what had once been

Challenger. Anything which could give a clue to the disaster would be needed.

Witnesses spoke of a tongue of flame near the base of the port booster rocket as the shuttle was throttling up to full engine power. Then a larger flame was seen near the base of the external fuel tank. Then came the explosion. There were contingency plans for rapid evacuation while the shuttle was still tethered to its launch tower – but it emerged that no one had prepared an escape route to be used once Challenger was airborne.

Until the explosion, routine dialogue was recorded between Challenger and Mission Control.

Mission Control commentator: '10-9-8-7-6, we have main engine start, 4-3-2-1 and lift-off. Lift-off of the 25th space shuttle mission. And it has cleared the tower.'

Pilot Mike Smith: 'Roll programme.'

Mission Control: 'Roger, roll, Challenger.'

Mission Control commentator: 'Roll programme confirmed. Challenger now heading down range. The engines are throttling down now at 94 per cent. Normal throttle for most of the flight is 104 per cent. We'll throttle down to 65 per cent shortly. Engines at 65 per cent. Three engines running normally. Three good fuel cells. Three good auxiliary power units. Velocity 22,057 feet per second, altitude 4.3 nautical miles, downrange distance three nautical miles. Engines throttling up, three engines now 104 per cent.'

Mission Control: 'Challenger, go at throttle up.'

Pilot: 'Roger, go at throttle up.'

Mission Control commentator: 'We're at a minute 15 seconds, velocity 2,900 feet per second, altitude nine nautical miles, range distance seven nautical miles.'

After an unexplained silence, the next words heard were from the NASA commentator: 'Vehicle has exploded . . . we are awaiting word from any recovery forces downrange.'

Months of inquiry followed. Former Secretary of State William Rogers chaired a presidential panel while NASA and the manufacturers of the shuttle booster, Morton Thiokol Inc, launched internal investigations.

Experts looked at the obvious possibilities of technical failure. A much earlier fear resurfaced, that the combination of the extreme weather and the shuttle's structure could have proved fatal. What sealed the fate of the Challenger and its seven crew on that bright January morning were vital rocket seals, never before put to the test in harsh, bitterly cold conditions.

The question of the rocket seals had been discussed the day before Challenger's fatal mission. Lawrence W. Wear, solid rocket motor project office manager at the Marshall Space Flight Centre in Huntsville, was in Florida for lunch. He called Boyd C. Brinton, manager of Morton Thiokol's project office in Huntsville who in turn called the Thiokol Wasatch Plant in Utah. There, the supervisor of rocket motor cases, Arnold R. Thompson, consulted with Robert Ebeling, the manager in charge of the solid rocket's motor ignition system and final assembly.

Ebeling sat down with Roger Boisjoly, of Thiokol's rocket-seal task force, and other engineers. They discussed how the shuttle would stand up to extreme weather no one had anticipated. The scientists wondered if previous incidents of booster-seal erosion had been directly linked to temperature. During a flight in October 1985, when the ambient temperature was 75°F, soot had been blown by a seal, which indicated a potentially dangerous situation. The same thing had happened again in January 1985, when launch temperature was 51°F. Roger Boisjoly argued there had been more visible damage to seals on the flight in colder weather. Thiokol engineers had calculated that the temperature of the internal rocket joints on that January mission was 53°F and that NASA could not afford to launch another shuttle in such cold weather, advice that was ultimately ignored.

At the time Challenger approached its final, fatal countdown the outside temperature was 36°F. Later, investigators discovered the temperature of the failed booster joint, chilled throughout the freezing night, was about 28°F at launch time.

According to Thiokol, the solid rockets had been tested and qualified for flight when the fuel temperature was between 40° and 90°F, but no separate guidelines had been established for more sensitive joints.

Roger Boisjoly had his own opinion. Cold weather made the seals, known as 'O-rings', less pliable. He was to say later that trying to secure a joint with a stiff O-ring was like 'trying to shove a brick into a crack versus a sponge.'

In Florida on the day before the mission, Allan J. McDonald, director of Thiokol's solid rocket motor project, was at the home of Carver Kennedy, vice-president of space operations at Cape Canaveral. Ebeling called McDonald there. He said his engineers were worried about the rocket seals and needed guidance. They wanted a further postponement of the shuttle launch, at least until late in the afternoon. NASA was not convinced. They wanted more people involved in the ultimate decision, and they were concerned about the mounting number of delays.

'They wanted scientific reasons for holding up the launch,' said Jack Kapp, a section supervisor of Thiokol. 'We had all made up our minds we should not fire.'

NASA was carrying out its own hasty research. Wilbur Riehl, chief of Marshall's non-metallic materials division, had been sent to look for data relating to O-ring performance in cold weather, but without much luck.

His colleague Robert Schwinghamer, director of the materials and processes laboratory, wanted tests done on the spot but Riehl didn't see how anything efficient and reliable could be done so quickly. 'We hadn't done any tests at low temperatures – or I'm pretty sure we hadn't,' Riehl said later. After searching, they came across reports indicating the rings were likely to be twice as stiff at 17°F as at room temperature – information that seemed to establish that weather was an important factor in rocket-seal performance.

'Should the outside temperature be lower than 20°F, we could be very uncomfortable,' Riehl pointed out. He said he had tried to alert Marshall's executives but the space centre chiefs were absorbed by a three-way telephone conference with other executives involved in the Challenger design and launch and didn't look at the newly discovered data.

At Cape Canaveral, Marshall booster manager Larry Mulloy stated that nothing in the data satisfied him there should be a launch delay. He was reported to have said: 'My God. When do you want me to launch – next April?'

George Hardy, science and engineering deputy at Marshall, said he was appalled at the idea of no lift-off. Later, he explained he was more concerned with Thiokol's presentation.

The Rogers Commission investigating the disaster concluded a seam in the booster rocket had failed but suggested strongly that there had been human error as well. Despite technical error which seemed to have haunted the rocket seal design for ten years, the commission reported, Thiokol engineers still had only a shaky understanding of how the crucial rocket booster joint performed, and of vital issues relating to launch temperature.

'Warnings were sounded and dismissed in these anxious pre-launch hours and the momentum preceding lift-off overpowered engineering concerns,' the commission found. 'Lacking hard evidence that a disaster was in the making, designers had to rely on their 'gut' feeling – not enough reason, in NASA officials' minds, to ground the flight. Management-level personnel, confronted with what they considered ambiguous data, opted not to rattle the chair of command. As a result, top NASA executives say they were unaware that the shuttle was flying against the advice of some of the very engineers whose careers had been dedicated to assuring its success.'

In harsh, practical terms, what had happened was that a seal on Challenger's solid rocket booster failed. Flames burst through a joint and then hit the ship's external fuel tank.

No technical jargon could bring comfort to Christa McAuliffe's family. Their sorrow turned to anger when evidence emerged that Challenger was doomed as a result of human error and not a technological fault.

Worse was to come. Everyone had believed that Christa and her fellow astronauts had died instantly at the time of the explosion. But weeks after the tragedy, Challenger's cabin and what was left of the crew was raised from the Atlantic ocean bed. This produced conclusive evidence that they had all survived at least several seconds after the explosion, and possibly until they struck the ocean surface.

William Shannon, former US Ambassador to Ireland, accused NASA of a cover-up. Why did it take them five weeks to find the sunken crew cabin? And five more weeks to bring it up from a depth of only 80 feet of water?

'The truth is the astronauts were alive and conscious for several minutes after the disaster occurred. They were probably making gigantic efforts to bring their craft under control. If the craft had been equipped, as it should have been, with ejector seats and parachutes, they could have saved themselves. There is a good chance they died only when their craft hit the water at 140 miles an hour and broke up because of the impact. They died because of NASA's false economies and incompetence,' stormed Shannon.

The Rogers Commission concluded the shuttle tragedy was due to mismanagement of the space agency. Challenger exploded because NASA executives ignored months of warnings about design and allowed the spacecraft to lift off in weather so cold it caused the O-rings between segments of its booster to fail.

The final technicalities no longer mattered to the 32,000 grieving residents of Christa's home town of Concord, New Hampshire. She was buried in the Catholic section of the town's public cemetery on 1 May, 1986 – exactly a year after the determined and adventurous school teacher of Concord High had declared: 'My philosophy is to get the most out of life as possible,' the statement that had won her NASA's teacher-in-space contest.

Her husband and children tried to carry on with their lives. Christa's mother came to live with them to help with the running of the household. A few weeks later, Steve flew to Louisville with the children to accept the Friend of Education Award, the National Education Association's highest honour – on Christa's behalf. He told 7,500 people at the convention: 'Christa was the most selfless person I have ever met. If you sit on the sideline, reflect on Christa as a hero, or as a glorious representative or a canonized saint, rather than putting your energies into accomplishing for her what she wanted to do, then I think her efforts will have been in vain.'

Then he flew back home with his children. He uttered no words of comfort for those responsible for the death of a much-loved wife and mother.

But the tragedy finally prompted aeronautical engineers to re-examine previous concepts. They modified the faulty joints and installed a heating system to protect them against extreme cold.

NASA developed a special escape system for its astronauts, who would henceforth have the final responsibility for allowing the launch to go ahead.

The improvements in design and human input were justified when the shuttle Discovery was launched on 29 September, 1988, while the world watched their TV screens, first in fearful anticipation, and then with sighs of relief as the graceful spacecraft soared up safely.

Flight KAL 007

The passengers aboard flight KAL 007 from New York to Seoul in Korea welcomed the chance to stretch their legs when the aircraft made its refuelling stop at Anchorage, Alaska.

The 246 passengers were mainly Korean, Taiwanese and Japanese, but included Americans, Canadians and Britons. With the crew of 23 on the long-haul flight to Korea, the Boeing 747 was carrying a total of 269 people.

It was 2.31 am American time at Anchorage, the busiest time of the airport's long night. The weather was dry that early morning of 1 September, 1983. There was a smell of autumn in the air.

The crew who left the Korean Air Lines flight at Anchorage to be replaced by three fresh flight deck personnel and 20 cabin staff were the lucky ones. It was the last day alive for all who took off on the last leg of the flight to Korea.

During that flight Captain Chun Byong-In allowed his craft to drift into Russian air space, even though his route was carefully mapped out. It was a specially sensitive flight, scraping the eastern border, and the off-course error proved fatal. The jet was blasted from the sky, mistaken by Soviet defence forces for an enemy aircraft. Flight KAL 007, with all its innocent people on board, became yet another casualty of war during peacetime, a political pawn whose fate caused anguished outrage throughout the world.

Captain Chun could not have been unaware of the danger of allowing his plane to deviate from the allotted flight path. He had a Russian-issued map clearly printed with the warning that the USSR reserved the right to shoot any aircraft that strayed too close to its military base on Sakhalin Island.

Every airline knew the Russians meant business. In 1978, another Korean Air Lines flight had violated Russian air space. The Boeing 707 was shot at, two passengers were killed and 13 injured. The plane was forced to make an emergency landing.

On the flight in 1983, neither passengers nor crew had any reason to fear that their eight-hour trip would provoke Russian retaliation. Captain Chun could not have failed to study his map and charts, but despite the warnings, he headed towards Sakhalin Island, a Russian military area.

The flight deck's inertial navigation system (INS) should have guided the 747 safely to its destination. An advanced computer programme pinpoints an aircraft's position accurately, and it was vital on flight KAL 007. But like all computer programmes, it relies on initial human input. If it had been incorrectly programmed after refuelling at Anchorage, it would have given a false reading. The INS has programmed 'way points', compulsory reporting points along the route. A minute before arriving at each way point, an amber alert warns the pilot he should get ready to report to ground to confirm his position. Two minutes later, the light goes off, to show the way point has been passed, and the pilot informs ground control of the time and position and estimated flight time to the next point.

The first major way point on the Boeing's route was a radio beacon at the hamlet of Bethel, 345 nautical miles away on the inlet of the Kuskowin River on the west Alaskan coast. As the plane made its way past this point, the captain reported normally. There was no hint of what was to come, yet the 747 was already 12 miles north of Bethel, and way off route. And as far as the captain and crew were concerned, the INS, linked to the automatic pilot which steers an aircraft on its proper course, was working perfectly.

But KAL 007 was by then heading dangerously towards Romeo 20, an air route which runs close to the Soviet Union's sensitive area of the Kamchatka Peninsula and Sakhalin Island. The area is under constant military radar surveillance by the Russians.

In the 747's cockpit, the INS appeared to guide the aircraft accurately towards its next way point, an imaginary aeronautical position called Nabie. By now the Korean plane was 40 miles north of its proper course. The aircraft continued to make reports at each way point, but unbeknown to its crew, the INS could not have been coupled to the autopilot. The early error would never have happened if it had been.

Passing another way point, the imaginary position of Neeva, the 747 had strayed 150 miles off course. The Korean Air Lines craft was now flying unannounced in an area supervised by Soviet civil controllers.

Ironically, the presence of another craft, a US Air Force RC–135, detected by radar, did not give the Russians cause for concern. It was not uncommon for such craft to patrol the area, sometimes as frequently as 20 days each month. What disturbed the silent Soviet watchers was the Boeing 747 flying 75 miles behind the American military aircraft. It was much too close to the Kamchatka Peninsula with its missile testing sites, and to the port of Petropavlovsk, a nuclear submarine base.

The Russians alerted six MiG–23 fighters which took off in hot pursuit of the unsuspecting 747. Somehow the pursuers missed their target. The Korean aircraft moved out of the Russians' air space for a while and the MiGs had to return to their stations. But instead of entering Japanese air space, the 747, now 185 miles off course, headed towards the south coast of Sakhalin.

This time the Russians were determined not to let their prey escape. They did not know whether the intruder was another US RC–135 or a Boeing converted into a fighter plane, or a civilian plane deliberately flying off course on a spying mission. Soviet fighters were again alerted to block its escape route.

The Japanese and American intelligence officers, aware of the Russians' monitoring system, assumed the Soviets were indulging in an air defence exercise.

Fighters from Sakhalin Island were also alerted. The Russians had just 10 minutes before the 747 would cross their air space and be lost to them.

Three fighters were involved in the mission. It was a pilot with the call sign 805 who announced to his control: 'I see it.'

Despite his identification call, the 747 did not respond, possibly because Russian systems are incompatible with those of other airlines. KAL 007 flew on, totally unaware that it was being lined up for attack. The pilot was still making normal procedural contact, now with Tokyo, for permission to climb to a higher flight level.

Fighter pilot 805 radioed: 'I am closing in on target.'

KAL 007 was now 365 miles off course.

As it received Tokyo's clearance to climb, fighter pilot 805 fired 120 rounds in four bursts, as a warning to the unresponsive and ignorant intruder. Even then, it seemed, no one aboard the Korean Air Lines jet realized what was happening. The Russian fighter fired his missiles. Seconds later, the plane with its 269 innocent people on board broke up, spiralling into the sea just outside Soviet waters. There were no survivors.

'The target is destroyed,' fighter pilot 805 reported to control.

The world was stunned.

The Soviet Union's act was denounced, and retaliation was demanded. The Canadians immediately stopped Aeroflot's flights into their country. Other nations followed suit. President Ronald Reagan closed Aeroflot's offices in New York and Washington. A worldwide 60-day ban was ordered on all flights to Russia.

At first the Russians refused to admit their error, but later they issued a statement admitting that the 747 had been attacked because it was believed to be a spy plane. The plane, they said, had not responded to a call for identification, after it had been tracked on radar for several hours.

At the time no one knew the Russians were planning to test a highly secret weapon on the night KAL wandered off course and were specially sensitive about intruders.

The reason why the Korean Air Lines jet made its fatal detour can only be speculated upon. It could have been straightforward INS failure. Failure of all three INS systems on board seems unlikely. Captain Chun may have switched off his INS control and forgotten to link it in again. No one will ever know. The cockpit recorder and flight data recorder boxes were never recovered.

One positive result of the tragedy was the improved communications between military and civil air controllers at Anchorage, Khabarovsk and Tokyo. But the plans to prevent innocent deaths in future brought little comfort to relatives and friends of those who perished. They could only grieve for victims of aggression in peacetime.

Great Scott

'For God's sake look after our people.' Those were the final, compassionate words written by one of Britain's most courageous explorers, Captain Robert Falcon Scott, on 29 March, 1912. With frostbite gnawing at his very bones, Scott lay dying in the bitter waste of the Antarctic. His tragic but heroic death ended a historic expedition. The world has forgiven him his error of judgment, but it has not forgotten his bravery.

Scott and his pioneering team of Dr Wilson, Captain Oates, Petty-Officer Edgar Evans and Lieutenant Bowers reached their goal, the South Pole, only to discover that a Norwegian team led by Roald Amundsen had already reached it. Amundsen hoisted the Norwegian flag and left two letters in a small tent. One was addressed to Scott, asking him to forward the other to Norwegian King Haakon, should his countrymen fail to return.

Yet the glory could have been Scott's, and Britain's. He could have got to the South Pole first and returned safely with his team to a hero's welcome. But it wasn't to be. Scott had made a fatal mistake during his preparations for his epic voyage to the South Pole. He decided to use ponies as his main form of haulage instead of dogs, which many thought were far more experienced, hardy and suitable. A small dog team went along only as back-up. This decision led to tragic consequences for Scott and his men.

Scott had upheld the family tradition by entering the forces. This pleased his father John Edward, whose ill health had prevented him from doing so. Instead he worked in a family brewery in Plymouth, taking a back seat while his brothers served their country. One was a naval surgeon, the other three were officers in the Indian Army.

Robert Falcon Scott was born near Devonport on 6 June, 1868. A governess taught him at home until he was eight, when he was sent to a day school. Later he went to Stubbington House, Fareham, Hampshire, before finally being entered as a naval cadet on the *Britannia*. He was just 13.

He joined the crew of the *Boadicea* as a midshipman, served two years there and then a short term on the *Monarch*. Afterwards he joined the *Rover*, one of the ships of the training squadron under Commodore Sir Albert Hastings Markham, the Arctic explorer, cousin of Sir Clements Markham, geographer and historian who, as president of the Geographical Society, was later to instigate the *Discovery* expedition.

Captain Scott before the start of the last expedition in 1911.

The young cadet could never have suspected that when Sir Clements came to the squadron as the guest of the Commodore he was already looking for a likely leader for the expedition to the Antarctic. But some time later, Sir Clements recorded one of their meetings. In his book, *The Lands of Silence*, he wrote: 'I had selected the fittest commander in my own mind in 1887. On the 5th, Scott dined with us. He was then 18 years of age and I was much struck by his intelligence, information and the charm of his manner. My experience taught me that it would be years before an expedition would be ready and I believed that Scott was the man destined to command it.'

Towards the end of 1888, Scott was transferred to the *Amphion*, then at Esquimalt in British Columbia. On the journey there he clearly displayed his leadership skills.

Because of bad snow on the railways he had to take a tramp steamer which was going to Alaska from San Francisco. The ship, packed with too many passengers, hit a mighty gale. Panic and chaos ensued, and women and children were lying prostrate with seasickness on the floor of the small saloon. Scott, a young sub-lieutenant aged just 20, took control. He organized the men – mainly rough Californian miners – into watches to wash, dress, feed and nurse the sick women and children. The men turned into a fairly disciplined crew, obeying his every order. Scott had shown flair at a very tender age for dealing with people and difficult situations.

He returned from Esquimalt a full lieutenant in 1891 and was posted to the *Vernon*, the naval torpedo school at Portsmouth, to specialize in torpedo practice, and finally to the *Majestic*, flagship of the Channel Fleet.

It was in June 1899, while on a shore leave in London, that he again encountered Sir Clements Markham. It was indeed a meeting of fate, recalled by Scott: 'Chancing one day to walk down Buckingham Palace Road, I espied Sir Clements Markham on the opposite pavement, and naturally crossed and as naturally turned and accompanied him to his house.

'That afternoon I learned for the first time that there was such a thing as a prospective Antarctic expedition; two days later I wrote to apply to command it.'

A year later his appointment as prospective leader of the expedition was announced. In June 1900 he was promoted to the rank of commander.

A sum of £92,000 was raised and the *Discovery* was built.

Scott was released from routine naval duties to superintend preparations for the expedition. It was thanks to his insistence, backed by the recommendation of high naval officers, that the ship's company, with the exception of the scientific personnel, was almost entirely recruited from the Royal Navy.

In the summer of 1901 *Discovery* set forth. The expedition surveyed South Victoria land, the interior of the Antarctic continent, rounded the Ross Sea and investigated the nature of the ice barrier. She returned in September 1904 after three years and three months.

Scott's reception was overwhelming. He was promoted to captain from the day of his return and was invited to Balmoral where he gave a lecture in the presence of the king, prime minister and other distinguished guests.

Foreign countries and their geographical societies awarded him their medals and decorations. *The Times* of September 1904 wrote of his work: 'It has been one of the most successful that ever ventured into the polar regions, north or south. True to the spirit of his instructions, he has done what he set out to do and even more. He has added definitely to the map a long and continuous stretch of the coast of the supposed Antarctic continent. His sledge expeditions, south and west and east, have given a part at least of the history of this land of desolation . . . Moreover, probably on no previous expedition has there been such unbroken harmony among its members.'

Scott's return on the *Discovery* that day heralded the beginning of the real expedition – when man would have to conquer the unknown, the vastness and harshness of the South Pole.

Scott was given nine months' leave to allow him time to record his first exploratory expedition. He had already written and sent home from New Zealand his report to the Admiralty.

His book, *The Voyage of the Discovery*, was finished in August 1905. Shortly before it was published Scott was appointed to a staff post as Assistant Director of Naval Intelligence at the Admiralty. Then came command of *Victorious* and *Albemarle* – and romance for Captain Scott.

After leaving the *Albemarle* in 1907, Scott returned to London. There he met a sculptress, Kathleen Bruce, daughter of Canon Lloyd Bruce of York. Their love blossomed and endured when he was posted to the battleship *Essex* in January 1908 and five months later to the *Bulwark*. In September that year, Kathleen and Robert married. He rejoined his ship after a short honeymoon at Etretat.

His comrades believed Scottie, as they called him, would now become a settled husband, abandoning all thoughts of a long, hazardous trip to the South Pole.

They were wrong. Plans were already being made for a new expedition. The British government and those of Australia, New Zealand and South Africa gave grants, but, inexplicably, the expedition was not an official one.

On the day Kathleen gave birth to a little boy, Scott was already working out his Antarctic goals. They were twofold: to undergo further exploration of the Ross Sea area and to reach the South Pole. He assembled the strongest scientific team ever recruited for polar work. Dr E. A. Wilson, who had been on the *Discovery*, was zoologist, artist and chief of staff. Dr G. C. Simpson, director of the British Meteorological Office, was meteorologist. There were biologists, geologists, a physician and a parasitologist.

On 1 June, 1910, the *Terra Nova* left the Thames under the command of Lieutenant Evans. Scott went on to the Cape of Good Hope in a mail boat. The expedition left Cape Town under Scott on 2 September for Australia and reached Melbourne on 12 October. Here Scott received a cable from the Norwegian Amundsen informing him that he, too, was about to make the attempt to reach the South Pole. Scott's heart sank. Did he have a premonition of the disaster that awaited him in the frozen wastelands?

The *Terra Nova* sailed for the ice from Dunedin in New Zealand on Tuesday, 28 November, 1910. His wife stayed on board until the ship was past the Heads, when a tug took her ashore. Kathleen and Robert held each other close upon parting. It was their last embrace.

Scott's intention was to find a landing place at Cape Crozier on Ross Island, but the heavy swell prevented this and he sought another landing place at Hut Point. It was here that his ill-chosen animal haulage team was landed.

Scott had decided not to take a full team of dogs, but had preferred to take Manchurian ponies specially bought in Siberia for the expedition.

He had insisted the ponies had to be white because he believed them to be more hardy than brown ponies. This delighted the dealers. The asking price for these rare beasts was sky-high.

Why Scott was adamant about using ponies remains a mystery. Earlier trips across the Antarctic ice had shown how vulnerable they were. But Scott would not be swayed. His obstinacy was to prove a fatal error.

By 12 January, 1911, everything needed for the expedition had been unloaded from the *Terra Nova*. Captain Oates had charge of the ponies. All stores for the Pole were first collected at a base named Safety Camp. Scott himself oversaw every detail and prepared to lay depots for his journey.

The *Terra Nova* left New Zealand before the beginning of the long Antarctic night, but not before Scott learnt that Amundsen's party was at the Bay of Whales, 60 miles nearer the Pole than he was.

The groups laid up for the winter between April and September – a long, frustrating night-time – and a start was made on 1 November, 1911.

The journey was in three stages – to the snow plain of the Ice Barrier, then to the Glacier and finally to the bleak, barren summit plateau of dry snow.

Plans were made to transport three units of four men to the Glacier. Two of these, as supporting parties, could help the polar party get within a reasonable distance of their goal.

The first part of the plan was carried out successfully. The two teams that went forward were led by Scott and Evans. By January 1912 they were getting closer. Petty-Officer Evans's party was sent back, with the exception of Lieutenant Bowers.

When Scott's team went on alone they were 120 miles from the Pole. Exhaustion began to take its toll for they were dragging heavy loads at over 10,000 feet above sea level. Progress was slower than anticipated and food was in short supply. Scott's realization that he had chosen the wrong animals to help lighten the burden of the arduous expedition came too late.

His men were hungry. As a dog-lover, Scott refused to kill and eat his dogs. During the drive to the Pole it was the ponies that were slaughtered to provide meat for both men and dogs – Scott's precious ponies, the very ones he had stubbornly set his heart on to help him make a success of his historic mission.

On 13 January, they still had 60 miles to go. The next day they covered 20. The dog team was dispatched back to the base camp. Now, as well as their own loads, the men had to pull the sledges too.

On 16 January, they experienced a feeling of triumph, then of despair. They had set off in reasonably good spirits, certain of reaching the Pole the next day. But on the last stretch of their journey, they came across the remains of a camp with a sledge track and the prints of dog paws. Amundsen, relying on his experienced dog teams, had been that way before.

In fact, his arrival, which marked him down in history as the first man to reach the South Pole, was 34 days before Scott's. Scott and his team dutifully continued until they reached the Pole, but they were despondent at evidence of the Norwegian victory. They knew it would be a bleak return trip. Food was even scarcer on the way back. Captain Oates and Petty-Officer Evans were early victims of frostbite. Wilson strained a tendon. Scott fell and bruised a shoulder. Somehow they managed to leave the tortuous plateau and reach the Glacier. Edgan Evans was by now very ill, and he died on 17 February. The four survivors struggled on, getting weaker by the hour. Then Captain Oates became seriously ill, his feet black with frostbite.

By the beginning of March the brave men knew the situation was hopeless – yet not one dared voice his gravest fears. Oates knew he was holding back his friends. He sought their advice. They said: 'Let's keep going together.' Wilson gave each man enough opium should a painless death be the only option.

On 15 March, brave Oates chose the ultimate solution without consulting his friends. He told them to go on ahead and let him sleep on. They would not hear of it. The thought of abandoning him to certain death was too much for the gallant band to bear. So Oates slept that night. He awoke to see a blizzard raging outside their tent. It was then he spoke the immortal words: 'I am going outside and may be some time.'

In a rare moment when he had the strength, when his hands had eased a little and the pain was not so bad, Scott wrote: 'We knew poor Oates was walking to his death, but though we tried to dissuade him we knew it was the act of a brave man and an English gentleman. We all hope to meet the end with a similar spirit and assuredly the end is not far.'

He was right.

The next day, Scott's right foot was completely eaten away by frostbite. He hardly noticed.

By 19 March, they had got within 11 miles of their food depot. But fate would once more dash their last, dwindling hope of survival.

Another blizzard blew up, blocking all attempts to push ahead. The men huddled together on 21 March to agree that Wilson and Bowers should go on, but they had to wait for the blizzard to die down. The heroic team were not to know it would keep tight its blustery, lethal grip for 11 days. They died before calm came to the Antarctic. Scott was still alive on 29 March, the day he made his sad last entry in his diary.

No one back home knew what had become of the men. It was eight months later, in November 1912, that searchers found the bodies.

Dr Wilson, it was reported, 'died very quietly with his hands folded over his chest.' Bowers lay 'in the attitude of sleep'. Scott himself lay between them, his left arm over Wilson, his oldest friend. His diaries were under his bag. Letters for Kathleen, his son and other close ones lay beside him.

The searchers did not disturb the bodies. There was something too moving about the sight of brave men, literally frozen in time.

A burial service was held and a pyramid built around the bodies. A cross was placed on it.

It was a tragic end – so near to glory, and yet so far.

Innocent victims

An American war plane homed in on its target – a fortification where Grenadian troops were believed to be stationed. But the fort turned out to be a mental hospital, and 50 innocent people died when the aircraft bombed it in error.

The tragedy happened during the US invasion of Grenada in 1983.

The Pentagon admitted the 139-patient hospital had been mistaken for the fortress, Fort Fredericks: 'Our personnel were unaware that a hospital was located at St George. Our troops observed the entire area was marked as a military area.'

Grenadian nurse Alice Celestine said later: 'We believe the Americans mistook the hospital for the fort when they saw the Grenadian army boys running towards it when the bombing started.'

A massive rescue operation was launched to find survivors in the rubble of Richmond Hill mental hospital in Grenada's capital of St George.

Rail disaster

Britain's greatest train tragedy ever occurred in the days when speeds were slower – but there was no advanced technology to ensure passengers' safety. Much of it depended on human judgement and efficiency. On one occasion, when that failed, five trains rammed into one another and more than 200 people died. It was a horror two men had to live with for the rest of their lives.

The morning air was still fresh as dawn broke over Quintinshill, Scotland on 22 May, 1915. Trains weren't running on time that morning, but that was not unusual. Scotland-bound expresses had left Euston station in London at 11.45 pm and at midnight and the two trains were expected to

115

approach Carlisle half an hour late. As was customary practice, a local train which normally followed them was sent on ahead to Quintinshill, where it was to be stopped to allow the faster trains to overtake it.

This arrangement was not new to signalmen Meakin and Tinsley.

When Meakin learnt of the local train's arrival, he had to decide where it could safely be shunted. The down loop already had a goods train from Carlisle standing there. So he directed the local train to the up main line. Business was getting a little too brisk, Meakin decided, especially when he was then asked to take on an empty coal train too. That went into the up loop. His last signal before handing the box over to Tinsley was to accept the first express train.

Both men only half listened when a message came that a special troop train carrying a regiment of the 7th Royal Scots from Larbert to Liverpool was making its way towards them on the up line.

For Meakin and Tinsley had been working a little fiddle between them. It had long been agreed that Meakin would tip off his mate Tinsley when the local train was stopping at Quintinshill. Tinsley would then take it from his home at Gretna Junction so that he could come on duty later than he should have done. While he was travelling down, Meakin would jot down train movements from 6 am onwards on a separate sheet of paper so that Tinsley could copy them into his train register, making it look as though he had never been late. Tinsley went on with his copying and Meakin settled down to read his newspaper.

No signal was ever sent to Kirkpatrick, where the coal train had come from, to say it was occupying the up loop. Staff at Kirkpatrick say what they did receive was a signal giving the 'all clear' for the troop train.

Tinsley went about organizing the expected trains.

At 6.38 am, he pulled off his down signals for the Scottish express. At 6.42 am he accepted the troop train.

He pulled off all his up main line signals. Three minutes later, the first of a double disaster shook the area as the troop train hurtled into the stationary local train.

Coaches from the local train were flung back 136 yards in the powerful head on collision. The engine was pushed back 40 yards. The engine from the troop train ended up lying on its right side across both through running lines. The 15 coaches of the troop train were smashed to pieces, the front ones shooting right over the engine and coming to land some distance in front of it.

Within moments a 15 coach train 213 yards long was crushed to almost half its size. It was carnage. But the tragedy had not ended. The second express train was making its way to Quintinshill.

Meakin rushed to the down signals to warn the oncoming train driver. A guard and other railway staff made a frantic dash along the line to give a warning. The driver could not believe anything was wrong. He was travelling at high speed under clear signals. Though he desperately tried to shut off steam when he saw the crazed waving in front of him, there was nothing he could do to pull up a 600-ton train in only 270 yards.

The express ploughed headlong into wreckage already littering the line. Survivors of the first crash, making a bid for escape, were felled as they ran. More people died as they tried to rescue other injured passengers. The troop train was struck again, right through the wagons of the goods train on the down loop. Coaches telescoped into each other.

The second smash had happened just one minute after the first. There were now five pulverized trains at Quintinshill – and barely nothing left of the troop train.

Eight people died in the second express train, and 54 were injured. Two people died in the local train. No one ever found out exactly how many perished on the troop train because the list of passengers had been destroyed. It was estimated about 215 soldiers and two railway servants died. About 190 men were seriously hurt. The accident inspector Colonel Druitt blamed the accident entirely on the 'inexcusable carelessness' and inattention to duty of signalmen Meakin and Tinsley.

Burnt-out coaches at Quintinshill after the collision.

They had made fatal mistakes that morning. Firstly, Meakin forgot to put safety collars on the signal levers controlling those parts of the line that had trains standing on them. These collars served as a reminder to the signalman and were designed so the levers could not be moved again while the track was occupied. The fireman of the local train, Hutchinson, had entered the signal box to check that this had been done, but Tinsley simply gave Hutchinson a pen to sign the book and carried on making the false entries in the train register.

Colonel Druitt also discovered the two men had overlooked the presence of the local train standing on the main line a mere 65 yards away in broad daylight. They had been too busy chatting with two brakemen who had popped in from the goods trains.

Hutchinson should never have left the box until he was satisfied the proper precautions had been taken to protect his train – the local which had made the fatal stop at Quintinshill that day.

The report stated that if the Caledonian Railway Company had installed inter-locking devices on signals at Quintinshill, the disaster may never have happened. But it was argued that the track layout was so simple that only human error could turn a relatively safe system into a lethal one.

It took almost 24 hours to extinguish the burning wreckage of the five-train pile up. Coals from the overturned engine of the troop train ignited gas cylinders used for lighting – and the flames spread with terrifying speed as the gas escaped under high pressure. Water was used from the tenders of the two goods trains but to little effect. A pump and hose were connected to a stream on a nearby farm to help fight the fire. The firemen from Carlisle arrived at 10 am. All that day and throughout the night the mighty train fire of Quintinshill raged.

When the fire fighters left exhausted at 9 am the next day, the 15 coaches of the troop train, four coaches of the express, five goods wagons and all the coal in the engine tenders had all gone up in the blaze.

The disaster happened because Meakin and Tinsley had not carried out their duties. Hutchinson deserved some of the blame, but it was the two signalmen who had to watch in horror as people died before their eyes in a tragedy of their making.

The horror led Colonel Druitt to introduce stricter safety measures. He strongly urged the abolition of gas lighting on trains, and recommended that steel rolling stock should be introduced, with more wrecking tools and fire extinguishers on all passenger trains.

Meakin and Tinsley could not fail to realize that these measures were the result of their own fatal carelessness.

Tampa Bay tragedy

'It was raining cats and dogs. It was dark. The wind was blowing like a hurricane. I was doing about 25 miles an hour, the Greyhound bus passed me doing about 35 miles an hour. As I came to the very top of the bridge I saw the rest was out. I applied my brakes within two feet of going in . . .'

The motorist, 60-year-old Richard Hornbuckle, was one of the lucky ones. For 35 people perished as their vehicles plunged 140 feet into deep waters in the great Tampa Bay tragedy. They were scattered like children's toys as a 600-foot ship ploughed into a massive section of the dual-carriage Sunshine Skyway Bridge linking St Petersburg and Florida's Central Gulf Coast of America.

The disaster happened on 9 May, 1980 as gale force winds and rain lashed the area. The *Summit Venture*, a phosphate freighter, was literally heading for a port in a storm.

'I was looking straight ahead,' the vessel's captain John Lerro was to recall later. 'I just didn't want to go barging through with all that rain. The next thing I saw was the bridge. It took me a moment or two to determine that it was not the centre of the bridge where ships are supposed to pass under.'

The Sunshine Skyway Bridge hit by the freighter *Summit Venture*.

119

What followed was the sickening sound of a crash and tearing metal as the freighter hit the bridge and brought down a 1,400-foot section of the Sunshine Skyway Bridge. For drivers making their way across the Tampa Bay span, there was little chance. All 21 passengers and the driver of the Greyhound bus were killed when it sank and became tangled in the twisted steel from the mangled bridge. At least five vehicles crashed into the waters.

John Lerro described his nightmare on that wild, windy day. 'Orders to reverse the engines and drop anchors were just too late. There was not time. The bridge fell down in sections, just seconds apart.' He had grabbed the ship's radio telephone and called the coastguard with a desperate Mayday alert. 'I looked up and saw the bridge was still falling. There were cars driving off.' Lerro said he considered dropping anchor before he reached the bridge but another vessel prevented him from turning left and leaving the channel. Turning right would put the *Summit Venture* broadside to the fierce wind and the ship would have been hard to control.

'The best thing to do was to head for that 306 foot gap,' the 37-year-old Lerro said, referring to the space between bridge piers on either side of the 600-foot wide channel. The empty, high-riding ship was pushed out of the channel by the wind. 'I felt sure she'd make the centre span,' Lerro said. But Lerro and his crew were misguided by buoys marking the channel, which seemed to 'appear, disappear then reappear on radar'. Seeing the buoys, Lerro thought he was on course and could safely pass under the bridge. But he was disastrously wrong.

Pulling out the dead from the mess of twisted bridge and crushed cars took three days. Each day brought divers the grim discovery of more bodies, buried deep under the wreckage. An eye-witness gave this graphic description of the mighty bridge that had toppled: 'The superstructure was torn and spread like a giant spider's legs against skies that were black and weeping.' A 56-year-old truck driver had a miraculous escape from death. Wesley MacIntyre was driving to work when he noticed the bridge 'swaying'. Then his truck hurtled into space, bouncing off the crippled ship and plunging into the swirling waters.

'As I approached over the high point of the bridge it started to give way. I couldn't stop. I just slid and hit the ship. Then I dropped into the water. I figured it was all over,' Wesley recalled. He escaped with a head wound and even managed to swim to the *Summit Venture* to be hauled aboard. He was the only survivor of those who were thrown from the bridge.

Today, locals of Tampa Bay and 14,000 commuters have a brand new, multi-million dollar bridge, but they are reminded daily of the tragedy of the original Sunshine Skyway Bridge. The death gap is still there, and grass grows on the approaches at either end of the sad structure.

CHAPTER SIX

ERRORS OF JUDGMENT

Simple errors of judgment have been the
cause of things going badly wrong in
countless walks of life since the beginning
of time. This chapter contains a heady
mix of some diverse examples of this,
including military blunders, elaborate
hoaxes, marketing fiascos and
misinformed murder trials.

Holy or hoax?

B elievers fell to their knees to give prayers of thanks when the news was announced. The Holy Shroud of Turin, the sacred cloth of Christ revered by millions, was to be displayed in public for the first time in 45 years.

The 14-foot length of linen was to be viewed on the high altar of Turin Cathedral in 1978, in a case with specially controlled atmosphere, to protect the precious religious relic from the slightest risk of damage.

In one month alone, more than two million pilgrims visited the cathedral to stand awestruck before this material evidence of the Crucifixion, miraculously preserved. The cloth showed the shadowy outlines of Christ's face, his eyes closed, and his forehead gashed by the crown of thorns. His arms were crossed and a mark on his right wrist showed where he had been nailed to the cross.

Ten years later scientists announced that the holy shroud, which had strengthened the faith of millions over the centuries, was the work of a 14th-century forger. Their pronouncement, backed by indisputable proof obtained by using the latest technology, ended long years of controversy and debate. Cardinal Anastasio Ballestero, the Archbishop of Turin, broke the news in October 1988. Technology had proved that millions of believers had been mistaken.

Scientists in Oxford, Zurich and Arizona had used carbon dating to check the age of historically authenticated samples of cloth and cuttings from the shroud and were '95 per cent' certain of their findings: the blessed item of Christendom was in fact a piece of linen woven between AD1260 and AD1390. It could never have covered the body of Christ. When the news was announced, Dr Michael Tite, keeper of the British Museum research laboratories, and Professor Edward Hall and Professor Robert Hedges of Oxford, all confirmed there could be no doubt about their scientific findings.

The news, though deeply disappointing to the faithful, did not come as a great shock to sceptics. As long ago as 1389, the Bishop of Troyes had described the shroud as a cunning forgery. He said his predecessor had met the forger!

The Holy Shroud which provoked so much Christian controversy over the centuries has a fascinating history. The first reference to its existence was found in St Mark's Gospel. The disciple stated that Christ's cloth was found in his empty tomb after the resurrection. Later, pilgrims to Jerusalem mention 'the shrouds of Christ'. It was later rumoured to be in Turkey, then in France and finally in the possession of the Savoy family in Italy during the 14th century. About this time, the first doubts about the authenticity of the mysterious and revered item were being expressed.

The Bishop of Troyes complained to the Pope of the time: 'Canons have falsely and deceitfully, being consumed with the passion of avarice and not for any motive of devotion but only of gain, procured for their church, a certain cloth cunningly painted, upon which by clever sleight of hand was depicted, the twofold image of one man, that is to say the back and front, they falsely declaring that this was the actual shroud in which our saviour Jesus Christ was enfolded in the tomb.'

In the late 15th century, the shroud was given for safekeeping to Louis I who built a chapel at Chambéry to house it. It was rescued from destruction in 1532 when fire gutted the castle, and was plunged into water. The signs of the burn marks are still visible. Early records show the shroud was once boiled in oil – but no one knows why.

The treasure was moved to Turin in 1578. Before its much publicized showing in 1978, the shroud had been taken from its hallowed casket on only five occasions. It was displayed for the marriages of Vittorio Emmanuele III in 1896 and of Umberto of Savoy in 1930. The third occasion was in 1933, a Holy year, marking the 1,900th anniversary of the death of Christ. When Italy entered the war, the shroud was hidden for safety in the sanctuary of Montevergine near Avellino in southern Italy. In 1946, the Archbishop of Turin cathedral, Cardinal Fossati, went to Montevergine to return the shroud to its rightful home.

In June 1970, the shroud had its fifth airing – at a secret gathering of Italians whose names were never revealed. They included an archaeologist, a chemist, a biologist, and church dignitaries. Dozens of photographs were taken and powerful microscopes were used to examine the cloth. The investigation was to herald many years of raging controversy and more scientific analysis.

The shroud's main surface is almost black, with the visible outline resembling a photographic negative, of a human face and body of a man 5ft 10½ inches tall. There appear to be bloodstains from the hands, feet, and a wound in the side. The torso bears the imprints of flagellation wounds and the eyes show the imprint of coins placed over them, a death ritual at the time of Christ. Early examination of the imprints revealed the coins had been minted shortly before Christ was crucified. This finding convinced experts in the early 1970s that the shroud could not be an ingenious hoax.

The Turin Shroud.

An amateur photographer, Secundo Pia, was allowed to take the now famous picture of the mysterious wrap in 1898. The photographic process created a clearer and more dramatic face, and Pia was greatly moved by what he saw. His photograph added more weight to the theory that this was indeed the linen cloth in which Christ's broken body had been wrapped for the three days before the Resurrection.

In 1931, the shroud was photographed again by a professional, Guiseppe Enri. The result convinced many more people that the shroud was indeed a holy relic.

And in 1981, American scientists using modern technology felt confident the shroud was authentic. Examination by experts in Santa Barbara, California, showed blood on the shroud to be human, but the Vatican would not allow them to use a special radiocarbon test which would have settled the issue conclusively.

In 1988, the Vatican finally gave permission for the carbon-14 tests to be done to date as accurately as possible the cloth, a blend of cotton and linen woven in a herringbone pattern. It was an earth-shattering decision.

The tests showed conclusively that the Shroud of Turin was not the burial cloth in which the body of Christ had been wrapped. It was the cunning fake of a 14th-century artist.

Even then, the results were contested by many who refused to believe they had been paying homage to a fake. Surely the same burst of energy which had resurrected Christ could have altered the composition of the cloth? Others felt the results confirmed their long-held doubts.

The confusion has been cleared up but the mystery remains unsolved: who perpetrated such a hoax? Was it the French knight Geoffry de Charny who 'discovered' the shroud in about 1350 and put it on display in the church he had just built? This would have attracted vast numbers of pilgrims – all willing to leave gifts in the collection plate. Even the great Leonardo da Vinci came under suspicion at one time. His genius was such that he could have easily fabricated a magical material – and myth.

'The church has nothing to fear from the truth,' declared the shroud's keeper, Cardinal Ballestero, before the results were announced. He stressed that the faith of the church did not depend on the shroud or any other religious relics.

Pilgrims and sightseers still flock to the Turin Cathedral in great numbers. 'I have been coming here for 30 years and nothing will persuade me that the holy shroud is not genuine,' said one.

Professor Robert Hedges, a scientist involved in the conclusive dating tests, commented: 'It is a shame that science gets involved in the testing of holy relics. It is like the loss of innocence in the garden of Eden, but once the question comes up, science has a responsibility to provide the answers.'

But belief is a powerful thing, and although a master forgery has been unmasked, it will make little difference to those who kneel before the Holy Shroud of Turin.

An ill wind for the jolly met men

It was the most devastating storm on record in Britain. Gales of up to 100 miles an hour swept the country killing 13 people, causing widespread destruction, uprooting hundreds of thousands of trees, robbing three million homes of electricity, and paralysing a quarter of the country. Yet only hours before, Britain's weathermen, equipped with all the latest technology, failed to warn the public.

Telly weather expert Ian McCaskill confidently predicted nothing worse than 'breezes' and 'a showery airflow'. BBC weatherman Michael Fish scornfully dismissed rumours of a storm brewing. 'A woman rang and said she heard a hurricane is on the way,' he told millions of viewers. 'Well, if you are watching and waiting, it isn't.'

A few hours later, meteorologists had to admit they had blundered badly.

The killer winds whipped up at 4 am on Friday, 16 October, 1987. There had been earlier signs of a strong gust, but no one alerted the country to what was to be the worst hurricane for 284 years.

Two fire officers on their way to answer an emergency call which turned out to be a false alarm were among the first victims of the storms. Ernest Gregory, 47, and Graham White, 46, died when an 80-foot oak crashed on to the cab of their water tender as they drove through Highcliffe, Dorset.

Patricia Bellwood was one of several people who were killed in their beds. She died when a chimney crashed through the roof as she slept at the Harte and Garter Hotel in Windsor, Berkshire. 'She probably never knew what hit her,' a policeman said later.

Firemen recovered the body of Ronald Davies as they cleared debris of the Queen's Hotel, Hastings, Sussex, which had blown down 'like a deck of cards.' Cyril Homewood, 59, died as the roof of his farmhouse in Biddenden, Kent caved in. Fisherman James Read was fatally injured when he was hit by a beach hut swept up in the gales in Hastings. In London, a tramp was crushed to death when the tree under which he had been sheltering toppled over. William Bennister is believed to have died as he tried to stop his garage doors from blowing away.

Road accidents provoked by the force of the gales claimed other victims. Sidney Riches, 37, from Highfield Farm, near Tottenhill in Norfolk, died on the A10 near King's Lynn. Police said his car collided with a lorry after first hitting a tree. James McCullum, 25, of Toxteth, Liverpool, was killed as his motorcycle was blown into the central reservation of the M62. Others died at the wheel of their cars as trees and debris crashed down. Two seamen from Singapore drowned after their British-registered bulk carrier capsized in Dover Harbour. There were lucky escapes too. The earth really did move for two couples making love during the storm. Winds howling at 90 miles an hour caved in the roof on Nikki Long, 23, and Matthew Dutton, 27, as they cuddled at home in Colchester, Essex. In Barnes, London, Aussie tourists Garry Buchan and Barbara Lewis only just fled their creaking camper van before a 30-foot tree flattened it. Said Garry: 'We've heard of being caught with your pants down, but this is ridiculous.'

Emergency services were unable to cope with the destruction. At the height of the hurricane, the London Fire Brigade was receiving a call for help every second.

Ships were sunk, a ferry ran aground, roads and railways were blocked with uprooted trees and farms were flattened. Houses had their roofs ripped off, tower block residents were evacuated, overhead cables were torn down. Hundreds of thousands of ancient trees were destroyed. 'It was as if a giant had walked through the gardens, kicking over everything in his path,' was how the curator at Kew Gardens described the devastation. Smashed, upturned trees stretched as far as the eye could see, each a unique part of the world-famous botanical collection.

In central London's three royal parks more than 1,000 trees were felled. A further 1,000 were lost at Hampton Court and Bushey Park. In Kent, the town of Sevenoaks lost six of the oaks it was named after.

Farmers counted the cost in millions of pounds. At one poultry farm in Essex, 17,000 birds died. In East Sussex, a tree fell across a building containing dairy cow and calf pens. Grain store roofs were ripped off as far north as Peterborough, Cambridgeshire. Recently harvested crops exposed to the storms were damaged, and power cuts disrupted milking operations

ERRORS OF JUDGMENT

After the storm.

and cold stores. Any fruit still left on trees had to be destroyed.

In the major horticultural area of West Sussex, between Worthing and Chichester, whole glasshouses were flattened. Damage in that part alone was estimated at nearly £3 million.

In the calm after the hurricane Britain was faced with massive transport disruption.

Commuter services were virtually at a standstill as more than 500 staff in the Southern Region toiled with army workers and volunteers to clear 5,000 trees from the region's lines. Over 170 trees lay across the 21-mile stretch of track between Tunbridge Wells and Battle.

More than 500,000 pupils from schools in London and the South-East stayed at home. Some school buildings had lost their roofs, temporary classrooms were blown away and playground walls collapsed.

Bus and railway stations were eerily deserted for a Friday as commuters stayed at home, trying in vain to call their workplaces on telephones put out of action by the storm.

Householders who had managed to sleep through the storm awoke to a landscape of both rural and urban devastation. Not even a reassuring cup of tea could be made as they considered their insurance cover. The electricity supply had been cut by the storm.

Sports fans were robbed of their pleasures too. Racing at Newmarket was called off – for the first time since 1908 – when the weather claimed another Newmarket fixture.

Head greenkeeper at the hallowed golf course at Broome Park near Canterbury, John Latham, viewed what had once been his pride and joy. Five greens had almost disappeared from sight, trees had been tugged from the ground, 12-foot holes gouged out of the turf.

Six craft were damaged at the Johnnie Walker world sailing speed record attempts at Portland Harbour.

Britain's top brass started to ask questions. Furious Tory MP Teddy Taylor described the lack of warning about the hurricane as 'incomprehensible'. Home Secretary Douglas Hurd chaired an emergency meeting on 'the storm crisis'. Prime Minister Margaret Thatcher and the Queen, both in Vancouver for the Commonwealth conference, wanted to return to Britain immediately. A state of emergency was declared as the full financial impact of the storms hit home. An estimated £200m worth of havoc had been wreaked. Insurance companies geared themselves up for a payout of £100m, the biggest single loss caused by a gale.

In the normally bustling City of London the Bank of England and the Stock Exchange closed down.

'It's the end of the world,' a gloomy stockbroker muttered sadly.

Why had there been no early warning of the killer winds, the nation demanded to know. The French Meteorological Department had been wide awake and had warned on the Tuesday of winds up to 90 miles an hour. Dutch television viewers were warned on Wednesday night of freak storms expected to hit the English south coast two days later.

At the European Centre for Medium Range Weather Forecasting in Reading, Berkshire, French scientists asked radio stations to put out a warning – but this was disregarded because it later contradicted with the British Meteorological Office computer at Bracknell, Berkshire.

The Bracknell computer had predicted a depression over northern France the day before the storm hit Britain. 'Later information is usually more accurate but in this case it was not,' said a rueful forecaster.

The storm had been caused by a collision between a belt of exceptionally humid air from the west of Africa and cold Arctic air drawn down over the Atlantic. The resultant depression, the worst recorded in Britain, deepened rapidly, passing west of the Brest peninsula and the Channel Islands, before centring on Britain in the small hours of the morning of Friday, 16 October.

The London Weather Centre issued a warning to the London Fire Brigade at only 3 am of a wind expected to reach a force of 80 miles an hour during the following hour. A spokesman at the centre admitted: 'We forecast strong winds overnight but nobody thought it would be anything like as bad.'

The British public made up its mind that night about the weather experts who had let them down disastrously, but it took a year to declare that the weather was no joking matter. The jolly television met men had to stop the wisecracks and concentrate on saving lives if abnormal weather was on its way.

The Meteorological Office in Berkshire responded by announcing the introduction of a computerized Amber Alert weather warning to be given to the police and other emergency services up to four days before bad weather was expected. A red warning would alert the public to dangerously heavy rain, snow, fog, blizzards and icy roads.

The system cost the forecasters £5m. They had learnt a costly lesson.

Dashed hopes

B rigadier-General Jean Louis Jeanmaire epitomized everything the Swiss Army could hope for in a top-ranking officer. He was fine, upstanding, honest and totally loyal to his country – the perfect patriot and soldier. When he retired the Swiss Government was proud to award him full honours.

Just 18 months later the same government learnt they had honoured the worst traitor in the history of Switzerland – a Russian spy.

The ending was not quite what Jeanmaire had planned and hoped for. It was a long way from his childhood when he dreamt of becoming a dashing, daring military man. He let his daydreams take him away from the reality of his strict upbringing in the Swiss town of Biel.

Jeanmaire knew he could make use of his degree in architecture to secure a commission as a regular army officer. In 1937 he joined the influential and elite unit of career officers, the core of the Swiss Army, who serve both as commanders of the country's home force and instructors in the reserve forces.

He was determined to win recognition by his superiors and missed no opportunity to air his views and to prove himself true and faithful to his country and the army. People listened respectfully when he listed the many virtues of Switzerland – and the evils of communism. By 1957 Jeanmaire had been made a full colonel and was becoming accepted in Switzerland's upper circles.

Then came the turning point. Although he had never seen action, he believed that as long as he was in the fighting force, he could consider himself a soldier with a reputation of courage and leadership in battle. His ideas were shattered when he was transferred to the civil defence forces.

Jeanmaire's personal life was desperately unhappy too. It was increasingly difficult for him to turn a blind eye when Marie-Louise, the woman he married 14 years before, flaunted her affairs. He was disappointed in his son, in whom he had invested more money than he could afford on the best schooling in an attempt to mould him into a satisfactory heir.

But soon Jeanmaire met the man who would change his life and lead him to betray his people and country.

Colonel Vassily Denissenko, the Soviet air attaché and a professional intelligence officer, greatly impressed Jeanmaire at a foreign diplomats'

131

gathering. Jeanmaire was surprised when the Russian telephoned him a few days later and invited him and his wife to dinner. That night an apparently warm and sincere friendship was formed.

As Jeanmaire came deeply under the influence of Denissenko he chose to ignore the fact that his 'friend' was sleeping with his wife.

The portly little Swiss colonel suffered another blow to his ego when a personal rival won the promotion to brigadier he had hoped for. That was when the Russians knew their prey was ready for manipulation. Denissenko moved in. He told Jeanmaire he felt he should make a greater effort to get to know other Swiss officers. Could Jeanmaire help? A few nights later Jeanmaire handed over a telephone directory containing classified listings of Swiss military personnel.

He knew he was breaking the law and violating highly sensitive army security. And the Russians knew there could be no turning back for their chosen traitor, but they wanted him to be fully aware of the power they had over him.

On one occasion Denissenko gave Jeanmaire an envelope crammed with money. The Swiss soldier reacted with deep felt hurt, and he screamed at Denissenko that he could not be bought. The Russians never had to offer Jeanmaire money again. They had his services for nothing.

Denissenko continued to ask his prey for more documents, more specialized army information. Jeanmaire's excellent memory enabled him to report almost verbatim to Denissenko the contents of official documents and files he was unable to steal, and his training as an architect was useful for drawing accurate and detailed sketches of military equipment and installations.

The Swiss Army expected Jeanmaire to meet foreign attachés and, because he was known as a life-long anti-communist, had no reason to suspect his liaison with Denissenko.

By 1964, the Soviet hold over Jeanmaire was such that there was no further need for Denissenko to work on him. He was replaced by Viktor Issaev who knew exactly how to handle the Swiss traitor: he flattered him as his equal.

Guilt began to gnaw at Jeanmaire. He threw himself into his army duties with renewed enthusiasm and his apparent devotion and commitment were rewarded in 1969 when he was promoted to Brigadier-General in charge of the country's civil defence forces.

By this time Jeanmaire's divided loyalty was making him ill. There was only one thing to do – tell the Russians he could no longer work with them.

They responded by sending in yet another Soviet attaché, Colonel Vladimir Strelbitzki, who had a different way of dealing with traitors.

When the frightened Swiss officer announced his intention to break off the relationship, the Russian threatened to expose him.

In return, Jeanmaire told Strelbitzki all he knew. The Russians learnt of the exact sites of missile targets, top secret fortifications, storage depots and command centres. Jeanmaire was valuable to them, because he was in a position to discover the weaknesses and scandals of prominent people which would make them vulnerable to Soviet blackmail when necessary.

Jeanmaire retired at the end of 1975, when he was 65, and delivered his last report to the Russians. He was awarded full military honours at a glittering retirement ceremony, and believed his evil past would somehow fade into oblivion, as he was doing.

But early on 9 August, 1976, agents of the Swiss secret service posted themselves near the Lausanne block of flats where Jeanmaire lived. They watched as the balding, solitary figure emerged for his regular morning walk. Then they pounced.

On 17 June, 1977, a Swiss court sentenced Jeanmaire to 18 years in prison, and to 'degradation and expulsion from the army'.

What led security officers to Jeanmaire? He desperately tried to find out. So did his lawyer during the trial. No answer was forthcoming from the grim-faced Swiss authorities. And who could blame them? They had successfully unmasked the man who gave his country away to an enemy – for nothing.

Dropping a bombshell

Millions froze in horror at the radio announcement – America was about to bomb Russia. They clearly heard President Ronald Reagan say: 'My fellow Americans, I am pleased to tell you I have signed legislation to outlaw Russia forever. We begin bombing in five minutes.'

President Reagan thought he was doing a sound check before taking part in an American radio show. He did not realize his little 'joke' had been picked up on audio tapes by radio stations across the country.

President Reagan's pointer.

White House Press Secretary Larry Speakes hurriedly called two networks, CBS and Cable News, to ask them not to disclose what had happened, but someone, somewhere, leaked the blunder, made during a warm-up to a Reagan broadcast. The world's press and TV made a meal out of the president's foolery, but Americans were by then used to Reagan's radio repartee. In a similar sound check two years earlier he had called the Polish government 'a bunch of bums'. During a visit to Venice, Reagan made a tasteless Irish joke, overheard by broadcast technicians.

The president always liked a little bit of innocent fun. As a young radio baseball commentator in Illinois, early in his career his link-up with a match broke down. So rather than have listeners switch to a rival station he invented a game and pretended to be continuing a live commentary.

The president often seemed to get it wrong. In November 1985, when he was involved in a cancer scare, he sort of forgot his own diagnosis. The growth taken from his colon was malignant, but he told a BBC interviewer firmly that it was benign. When the BBC collected the tape from the White House the error, though fiddled with by Reagan's staff, could still be heard.

In Brazil, Reagan told baffled dinner guests how pleased he was to be visiting Bolivia. Receiving Lee Kwan Yew of Singapore at the White House he bade him 'Welcome to Singapore Mr Yew.' He gaily addressed President Doe of Liberia as Chairman Moe, and called the boxer Sugar Ray Leonard and his wife 'Sugar Ray and Mrs Ray'. Reagan often forgot his official lines and replaced them with the script of one of his old Hollywood movies instead. Once, when presenting medals of honour, he recalled as fact an act of bravery he had performed – but only on celluloid in an old film called *Wing and a Prayer*.

As a young governor, Ronnie Reagan predicted confidently: 'I just wanna say the Beatles have as much chance of getting the MBE as I have of becoming President of the United States.' He was destined to eat his words.

Battle of Blenheim

For more than two years the War of the Spanish Succession had been raging in Europe between England, Holland and Austria on one side, and France, Spain and Bavaria on the other.

Now both sides were preparing for a decisive battle in which England was determined to rid its Austrian allies of the marauding French. It was the Battle of Blenheim, and the French may well have been able to stand their ground and claim a historic victory had it not been for the blunders of the French Marshal Tallard.

The Duke of Marlborough had in fact expected the French under Tallard's command to win. Instead, the French leader simply goofed off.

On the evening of 12 August, 1704, the English were very uneasy. Their enemy, the French, had advanced almost as far as Austria's capital Vienna.

The Duke of Marlborough realized that Austria had to be saved, for without her help England would never win the war. He planned a daring stratagem. At the beginning of the year the Duke had led his army away from the Netherlands and into the heart of Germany, conquered Bavaria and joined the Austrian army under Prince Eugene in preparation for a great attack on the French. The French had been completely hoodwinked by

Marlborough's daring march and it was not until he was well on the way to the River Danube that it was realized he was marching to relieve Vienna. A French army hurried to the defence, teaming up with the Bavarians, and established their camp near the village of Blenheim to await the approach of their enemies.

The scene for the Battle of Blenheim was set.

The armies of Marlborough and Prince Eugene had halted to the north-east of Tapfheim, a small village close to Blenheim.

The Duke was studying a roughly marked chart in his tent. He knew if he failed, his country would be in danger from the French, and he himself would be ruined.

Prince Eugene joined him to discuss tactics. One thing they both agreed on was that their enemy leader, Marshall Tallard, would make mistakes. This gave them some hope of victory.

At dawn, on 13 August, the morning mist prevented the French and Bavarians from obtaining a clear view of the approaching armies, but later, when it cleared, they realized the hour of reckoning had struck.

By midday, Marlborough had reached a river, the Nebel, which flowed across the plain into the River Danube and separated the opposing armies.

Blenheim was packed with soldiers under the Marquis of Clérambault, who hoped to make an attack on the rear when the English advanced. Marlborough had anticipated that the French would occupy Blenheim and had already issued instructions to make an assault on the village as soon as the battle began. Meanwhile, Prince Eugene was making slow but steady progress through the wooded country to the west to take up his position on the right wing opposite the forces from Bavaria.

The signal was given and Marlborough's army advanced. At first the French fought back fiercely, weakening their attackers' line as men fell dead to the ground. But as the fighting continued, reinforcements swelled the English ranks and the French were driven back inside the village.

Now Marlborough took advantage of a great tactical error made by Marshal Tallard. He had reached the opposite banks of the Nebel, where Tallard cunningly offered no resistance while his enemies crossed the river. His own scheme was to launch an attack on the English before they had time to line up after reaching the other side and then to drive them back to the adjoining marshy lands.

The tactic failed dismally. Although the French army leader did in fact give the order for a charge to be made, Marlborough's army was prepared to stand its ground against the attack.

Then Tallard made a fatal error. He left the scene. His inexperienced men had to carry on the defence as Tallard foolishly went to see how the fight against Prince Eugene's forces was progressing. Unfortunately, he decided to take the Marquis of Clérambault's 3,000 fighters with him.

The Duke of Marlborough took full advantage of the confusion among his enemies. He determined victory would be his before nightfall, and mustered his army for a final attack. Thousands of panic-stricken French soldiers scattered. It was too late for Marshal Tallard to try to regain command of the fearful army. He was among those forced to surrender, and was taken prisoner.

Among those who died was the Marquis of Clérambault, who abandoned his men in Blenheim and plunged to his death in the waters.

The hapless Tallard was treated with courtesy by his enemy despite his military blunders. He was even taken in the victorious Duke of Marlborough's coach from the battlefield under escort, and sat out the bumpy journey in despondent silence. He had handed the British victory on a plate.

The most expensive hole in the world

It was the biggest hole ever dug – and at £14 million the most expensive. And because no one wanted it, it had to be filled in again.

The saga of the unwanted hole began in 1973, when the Department of Energy under Anthony Wedgwood Benn, decided to capitalize on the fast growing North Sea oilfields. What was needed, the department felt, was giant concrete oil platforms which would require massive excavation work.

The area earmarked for the innovative construction work was picturesque Portavadie overlooking Loch Fyne on Scotland's west coast.

Not only was the location a bad choice, but fate was against the project. The roads leading to the isolated hamlet were poor, and someone should have noticed that the outlet from the loch to the sea wasn't deep enough to accommodate any oil platform, concrete or not.

137

The government had grossly overestimated the demand for its massive £250-million platforms. And just then, the oil industry took a dive. No one wanted oil platforms, the government had to admit.

You couldn't blame one elderly resident of Portavadie for being particularly upset. Miss Munro had had to move her sheep off what had once been fine pasture land and all she had for her trouble was a hole 450 yards long and 50 yards wide. 'My view has been spoilt,' she said, somewhat politely under the circumstances.

Another victim was farmer Robin Watson, hired as transport manager for the ill-fated project. His efforts had been all in vain. The excavation work cost £11 million and a further £3 million was spent on constructing a village for the 700 workers involved in the project. But no one actually lived there. In 1976, the government conceded defeat.

Robin Watson explained: 'They never issued a compulsory purchase order on the village, even though it was built with government money. And under Scottish law the buildings belong to the landowners.'

The village was eventually sold off to a mysterious off-shore company in Curaçao – and resold days later to another company based on the South American island.

The Department of Energy and the Scottish Office came in for a drubbing from the Commons Public Accounts for squandering 'substantial sums' of public money.

But that was not the end of the world's costliest cavity. The bulldozers moved in again. They breached the sea wall and the waters of Loch Fyne flooded in to fill what was now known as Benn's Black Hole. Landscapers arrived to try to restore the shoreline to its original state. That was to cost taxpayers another £1 million.

But for Miss Munro, who had seen the area she'd lived in all her life spoilt for ever, the money was not important. 'It will never be the same again,' she said sadly, from behind a line of washing carefully placed to block out the blot on her view.

Amy

Air ace Amy Johnson became a legend in her own lifetime, hailed around the world for her brave pioneering flight from Britain to Australia, when she was 26, in May 1930. A heroine's welcome awaited her in Melbourne when she landed there after her epic 19-day flight in her single-engined, secondhand Tiger Moth.

Yet this intrepid pilot, whose courage and determination were legendary, inexplicably ran out of fuel on a short flight from one British airfield to another. The mistake cost her her life and she plunged to her death in the icy waters of the Thames estuary on 5 January, 1941. No one could understand how a pilot as skilled and experienced as Amy Johnson could have made such a basic, fatal error.

Amy had taken off from Squire's Gate airfield near Blackpool earlier that day to deliver a twin-engined RAF Airspeed Oxford to RAF Kidlington in Oxfordshire. It was a vitally needed wartime aircraft and Amy was well aware of the importance of her official Air Transport Auxiliary mission.

The weather on that day in midwinter was not ideal for flying, with a dangerous inversion of warm air above cold air. This could have caused her aircraft to ice up dangerously and as an experienced pilot Amy would have flown at a higher altitude than normal to rise above the bank of cloud covering the country.

Experts later pieced together the sequence of events leading up to Amy's death plunge. When she reached Oxfordshire, she would have known that there were hills and radio masts which posed a hazard to low-flying aircraft. She would not have been able to drop any lower, and the presence of cloud would have made it dangerous for her to attempt to get her bearings visually.

There is little doubt that Amy's best bet would have been to turn east to head for her usual base at Hatfield. She knew the area well and from there she would have been able to fly on to southern Anglia's flat lands and drop safely lower under the clouds to plot her onward course.

The next news of Amy came when rescuers fished her body out of the lonely Thames waters. She had baled out, but instead of parachuting safely to the ground, she had plummeted into freezing water, too shallow to allow rescuers to pick her up by boat, even though valiant efforts were made to reach her. One man died in the attempt.

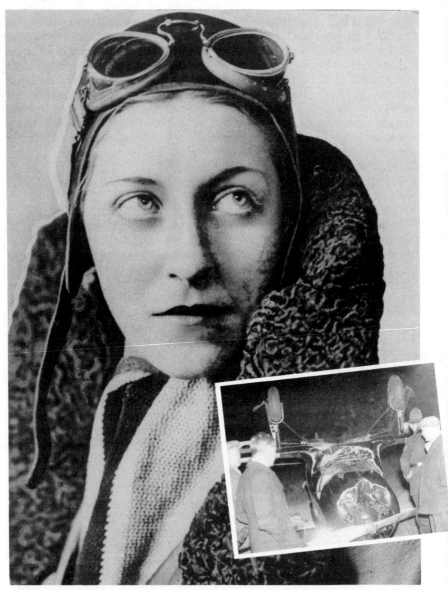

Amy Johnson and the plane in which she made her last flight.

The fuel gauge in her aircraft showed empty, which explained why she had had to bale out. Tragically for her, she mistook a line of barrage balloons stretched across the seven-mile width of the estuary for a land marker.

She ran out of fuel because she had been flying for four and a half hours, the maximum range of an Airspeed Oxford without refuelling. It is likely that Amy got herself lost in poor visibility and was too proud or stubborn to turn back, but no one will ever be able to confirm this scenario, or be sure about the motive that drove her on while the indicator on her fuel gauge dropped inexorably. There is no record that she made any attempt to land and refuel.

It seems likely that her unnecessary, tragic death fulfilled a macabre wish for the introverted air ace. She suffered most of her life with depression over love affairs that had turned sour.

If one relationship in particular, with a Swiss businessman she met when she was 18, had gone well, Amy would not have taken to the air in the first place. But her love married someone else and Amy, with the twisted reasoning of a woman scorned, decided to take up flying, a dangerous activity which, she was well aware, could easily kill her. It was the most dramatic way she could think of to make her hurt and rejection known.

So she became a pilot and a pioneer, risking her life, and winning fame and adulation. And eventually her bitter wish came true.

The dingo baby trial – and error

The early evening sun beat down on the Australian desert resort and holidaying campers were happily making preparations for a barbecue under the welcoming shade of a few trees. Suddenly, the heart-twisting screams of a frantic woman rent the air.

'A dingo has taken my baby!'

Those words were to launch a macabre, chilling Australian murder trial which held the world spellbound for several years. The 'Dingo Baby' story began as a terrible family tragedy, turned into a mystery, and finally ended when a mother jailed for killing her own infant was freed – after the mysterious death of a young man.

The scene of the drama was the mystical Ayers Rock area in the centre of the Australian outback, the site of ancient and powerful aboriginal rites and beliefs. Over the years the rock, a natural world wonder, has exercised a strange fascination over visitors from all parts of the world.

The leading character in the drama was Lindy Chamberlain, whose terrified screams were heard at the campsite on 17 August, 1980. Her husband Michael, a Seventh Day Adventist pastor, played a supporting role in an eight-year nightmare which threatened to destroy the family after the mysterious disappearance of their baby daughter, nine-week-old Azaria.

The Chamberlains' ordeal of trials – and grave error – ended in September 1988 when Lindy was freed after 40 months' imprisonment for allegedly murdering her baby with a pair of scissors. The costliest trial in Australia's legal history involved five gatherings of legal and forensic experts whose findings at first condemned a mother for allegedly slashing her own baby's throat, and later set her free as an innocent woman.

Lindy Chamberlain's own unwavering version of the tragedy was that a vicious dingo, an Australian wolf dog, had seized baby Azaria as she slept in her cot in the family's tent. She maintained that the dingo had gripped the child's head violently between its teeth and had dragged her off to its lair. All that remained was the infant's pathetic shredded, blood-drenched jump suit. The matinée jacket Lindy swore the baby had been wearing at the time could not be found anywhere.

142

The infant's disappearance prompted a search of the area in which 300 people took part without finding a body.

Alice Springs coroner Des Sturgess found at the first inquest on Azaria's death that 'Mr Chamberlain went to the barbecue area and was there for some considerable time in the presence of witnesses when Mrs Chamberlain cried out "A dingo has got my baby!"'

'In the time they went to the campsite and the time Mr Chamberlain was at the barbecue area, the death was caused.'

That was the only hard fact which could be established during the inquiries which were to follow.

Lindy and Michael Chamberlain believed the first inquest would end their ordeal, since they had been cleared of any blame in the tragedy. But a year later, the nightmare began all over again.

The Northern Territory police in Australia were not happy with the coroner's findings. They produced new forensic evidence which was laid before a second inquest in 1981.

The incriminating evidence Sturgess now had to consider was a woman-sized handprint on the baby's clothing and evidence that the baby's little suit had been handled with hands wet with blood.

Blood was to play a large part in implicating 33-year-old Lindy and her 37-year-old husband in a crime they did not commit. Blood was found on the door handle of the Chamberlains' car, under hinges, on the carpet and under the dashboard – in places not clearly visible or accessible, the experts stated. Some of the traces were fetal blood, consistent with that of a baby's.

Blood traces were also found in a camera bag belonging to the Chamberlains, in 'nooks and crannies' and on the clasp. There were minute bits of baby hair in the bag.

British forensic expert Professor James Cameron of London Hospital Medical College had been called in. His theory was that Lindy had slashed her baby's throat, possibly with a pair of scissors, as she sat in the front seat of the car. The baby's jump suit, recovered several days later behind the camp site, showed evidence that the child had been held by human hands: the bloodstains were not consistent with an animal's attack, the experts maintained. There were no signs, the inquest heard, of saliva or fur on the clothes. Although the body has still not been found, the sum of the evidence pointed an accusing finger at Lindy and Michael Chamberlain. On 2 February, 1982, at Alice Springs, coroner Gerry Galvin ordered Lindy to stand trial for the murder of her baby Azaria, and indicted Michael as an accessory.

Even before the sensational trial started, horrified followers of the macabre story were convinced of the Chamberlains' guilt. Their case was

The Chamberlains after the charge of murder was made.

further weakened when both inquests revealed that Ayers Rock was a sacred site used for centuries by aborigines in initiation and childbirth ceremonies, and that Lindy and Michael had visited other aboriginal sites in the same area. These included a site called Cut Throat Cave.

Because of its sensational and controversial aspects, the authorities decided the trial should be moved from Alice Springs to Darwin where the jury was more likely to be impartial.

The trial began on 19 April, 1982. The Chamberlains had been granted bail of £3,000 each. The next seven weeks were to make Australian legal history as a jury of nine men and three women listened intently to evidence which first damned, then exonerated the couple, then provoked a six-hour summing up by Mr Justice James Muirhead. The evidence of campsite witnesses, forensic scientists, lawyers and police, was led. Professor James Cameron stood by his initial claim. He said that, from the state of the baby's jump suit, death had been caused by an incised wound on the baby's neck, in other words a cut throat, inflicted with a cutting instrument across or around the neck held by a human element.

Prosecutor Ian Marker accused Lindy of killing her baby, burying the body in the desert and then, with her husband, digging it up again to remove the clothing and place it near a dingo lair. Lindy's dingo story was a 'fanciful lie' he said.

The defence called 28 witnesses, including 10 who said Lindy had been loving and caring towards Azaria and one holidaymaker said Lindy had a 'new mum glow about her'.

Two witnesses gave evidence that the day before the baby disappeared two other children at the campsite were confronted by a dingo that showed no fear and grabbed the seat of a teenager's trousers. Another said a dingo had seized her six-year-old son by his bottom, causing bad bruising, teeth marks and bleeding. A month before Azaria's death, a dingo was shot as it tried to snatch a three-year-old child from the seat of her parents' car.

It was also considered unlikely that Lindy would be able to slit her child's throat, wash her bloodied hands and return to join her husband at the barbecue site in the ten minutes she was absent.

There were gasps in court as another witness, Kyth Lenehan, told that he had been in an accident in June 1979, and the kindly Chamberlains had taken him in their car to hospital. He had bled quite heavily from a head injury.

During the trial, the entire court was flown to the death scene at Ayers Rock. Two women jurors wept during the proceedings when shown the baby's bloodstained clothing – Lindy wept too. Films were shown of a dingo snatching a doll, savagely gripping its head between its teeth.

Melbourne consultant biochemist Finely Cornell said blood samples were less reliable when examined a year after the blood was shed, as had happened with the second inquest evidence.

He stated that six samples of carpet taken from the Chamberlains' car bore no traces of blood at all, and that the baby's jump suit, singlet and nappies had marks consistent with those made by dingo teeth.

Dr Hector Oram, reader in dental surgery at Melbourne University, said the holes in the baby's clothes were consistent with those in material bitten by dogs and dingos he had examined.

Things looked very good for the Chamberlains. The jury was out for a long time. Lindy and Michael displayed no emotion when they were declared guilty.

Judge Muirhead told Lindy: 'You have been found guilty of murder and there is only one sentence I can pass upon you within the law of this territory and that is imprisonment with hard labour for life.'

Michael was found guilty of being an accessory and was given 18 months suspended sentence, and was bound over in the sum of £300 to be of good behaviour for three years.

Lindy's sentence caused shockwaves, not only because she had been found guilty of slaying her own child, but because she was eight months pregnant when sentence was passed on 29 October, 1982.

An appeal was immediately lodged. Lindy gave birth to another little girl, Kahlia, in prison, two days before she was freed on bail pending the appeal.

Conditions of bail were that she lived with her husband and sons Aidan and Reagan and her parents at a Seventh Day Adventist Church in northern New South Wales.

On 30 April, 1983, Lindy's appeal was rejected. She was delivered back to Berrinah jail in Darwin to 'resume her sentence as soon as possible.'

She lost a second appeal the following year and seemed destined to spend the rest of her life working in the prison laundry.

Then came a dramatic twist which was to clear her name at last. In February 1986, by an almost psychic coincidence, climbers searching for the body of a British tourist who had jumped to his death on Ayers Rock found Azaria's bloodstained matinée jacket in an inaccessible place where the couple could not possibly have placed it. Police were later to find 'organic material' near the jacket which could have been the baby's remains.

This was a blow for the prosecutors who had steadfastly maintained that the jacket Lindy claimed had gone missing in the dingo snatch was a figment of her imagination. But the sad little garment corresponded exactly to the description she had given police at the time of the inquiry. Lindy was freed from prison to allow her to have access to legal advisers to prepare yet another inquiry.

In May 1986, the Royal Commission Inquiry began 11 months of proceedings. Heading the inquiry, Mr Justice Morling found many faults with the case presented by the couple's accusers. He blamed unreliable and wrong forensic evidence, and said important witnesses had not testified at the trial. 'Bloodstains' under the family car's dashboard had probably been caused by an insulation problem, Judge Morling found.

The couple were granted a pardon.

But this was not enough for Lindy: 'There is no satisfaction in getting a pardon for something you didn't do in the first place.' She and Michael wanted the world to know they were not to be forgiven for a horrendous crime they didn't commit. They wanted their names cleared once and for all.

The legal wheels were set in motion once again while Lindy and Michael were reunited and picked up the pieces of the long months apart during which he had cared for their three children.

'Lindy is quite new to me even though we lived together for 13 years before all this happened,' Michael told the world.

Lindy spoke of her time in jail. Of how she feared violent action from fellow inmates; of her vegetarian diet and her jogging to keep fit; of the prison slang; the rules. 'If you let your self-esteem go, if you lose your self-respect, you lose your grip on everything else. I didn't. I'd fight first.'

On 15 September, 1988, three judges in Australia declared Lindy and Michael completely innocent. They immediately went into hiding to pray.

Said Northern Territory Senator Bob Collins: 'This has been the gravest miscarriage of justice ever experienced in this country. The Chamberlains' reputations have been destroyed. One thing I hope is now going to come out of it is that there are enough fair-minded people about to say "Well, yes. We were wrong."'

It took just ten minutes for a packed court in Darwin to declare Lindy and Michael Chamberlain had never committed any crime. As soon as the verdict was announced, the couple's lawyer announced he would institute further proceedings – to win compensation for all the years they had lived under sentence of killing their own baby, whose name meant 'Blessed of God'.

In a television interview Lindy gave at the height of the Dingo Baby headlines, she said: 'If you've ever seen dingoes eat, there's no difficulty for them to remove clothes. They never eat the skin. They use their feet and hands and pull back the skin as they go – just like peeling an orange. I knew my baby was dead. It was God's will.'

If the public had believed what Lindy had claimed all along, the nightmare would never have been, and the Australian taxpayer would have been £15 million richer.

Slip-up

Russian manufacturers were tripping over themselves to live up to their leader's demand that all Soviet goods should be of first-rate quality. But one hapless shoe factory slipped up on the job by sending out a strange batch of boots which had high heels attached to the toes.

The Russian people saw the funny side of it. Mikhail Gorbachev didn't. And the tipsy-toed footwear was put on show in the Ukraine to shame the shoddy shoemaker.

Return to sender

The whole world warmed to the story of a little boy called Buddy who was fatally ill with leukaemia. The plucky eight-year-old had expressed one last desire: he wanted to earn a place in the Guinness Book of Records by collecting the largest number of postcards in the world.

It was a moving wish, one even the American President couldn't ignore. Ronald Reagan wrote a letter of encouragement to Buddy in Paisley, Scotland. The touching story soon spread around the world. Scandinavian newspapers and television companies organized appeals on Buddy's behalf. Australia joined in; the Canadian Navy printed Buddy's address in its monthly house magazine to circulate it to forces worldwide. In Britain, a note about Buddy was pinned up on a House of Commons notice board. It appealed to MPs and their staff to become involved.

Cards of all sorts flooded in at a rate of 20,000 a day – until it was discovered that Buddy did not exist. The whole charity project had been a waste of time. It had started in all innocence when Cameron Black, a retired security officer from Paisley, heard Buddy mentioned on the crackling airways of a citizens' band radio in 1982. Someone had said that a little boy dying of leukaemia was collecting the special 'eyeball cards' CB enthusiasts send to each other after making contact on the air.

Without feeling the need to check it out, 60-year-old Cameron Black offered his own box number as a mailing address for the cards. Within a few months he had 180 bags of mail clogging up his house. Eventually he became uneasy about his errand of mercy. When he called hospitals and schools throughout Scotland they could find no trace of a child called Buddy. By then, the whole thing had got out of control.

Only Britain's hard-pushed Post Office knew the score, after handling a similar appeal for a non-existent eight-year-old called Mandy who was said to be mentally handicapped and wanted to acquire a record-breaking card collection too. When Buddy's appeal started to snowball, sorters shook their heads again. The cards were marked 'return to sender' or burnt.

Officials checked and found out that the *Guinness Book of Records* had never included an entry for the greatest number of postcards collected by one person. 'Buddy has become a pain in the neck,' a spokesman for the publishers said. But the little boy who never was had also become famous.

The finger of suspicion

It was a gruesome discovery and the finger pointed firmly at foul play. Twenty policemen with tracker dogs scoured the Bristol countryside looking for the body to whom the severed finger found in an adventure playground belonged.

An experienced Home Office pathologist had stated categorically that the finger belonged to a body that had been dead for a month. The severed digit was sent for further tests while police officers pressed on with their hunt.

Back came the report: 'It's a joke finger!' Police at Bristol were reluctant to reveal the name of the man who had sparked off the Bristol murder fears, but semi-retired pathologist Dr Derek Johnson 63, admitted: 'Oh dear. This is extremely embarrassing. The finger was given to me in a very casual way and I did not make a full examination.'

He had picked it up, he said, turned it over and had only a brief look. It appeared to be a mumified human finger; the skin seemed elastic and a bone was missing. 'I did say you couldn't state exactly how old it was but that it would take a human finger about four weeks to look like that,' Dr Johnson explained. 'But I was puzzled there was no blood.' He added that it was a very sick joke to play on anyone.

The finger had been found one Sunday by a woman out for a stroll, and was examined by a local fox expert, Dr Stephen Harris from Bristol University. He, too, thought a ghastly deed had taken place and that a fox had later torn the finger off a dead body. 'It looked realistic, but it did in fact remind me of a rubber joke finger,' he said. 'But it stank to high heaven so I didn't want to look too closely.'

Police called off the hunt.

The Sinclair C5

No one had seen anything quite like it. Right from the moment the Sinclair C5 was unveiled, on 10 January 1985, by its balding, bespectacled creator, Sir Clive Sinclair, the little battery-powered tricycle created controversy.

The idea seemed a good one at the time. Manufacturers had been scratching their heads for years trying to develop a motor vehicle which was quietly electrically-powered, pollution-free and cheap to run and Sinclair's C5 seemed to fit the bill perfectly. The three-wheeler had a top speed of 15 miles an hour, a lead-acid battery providing a 20-mile range and a compact, plastic, light-grey body.

For the £399 purchase price you also got a battery charger and a safe-driving book from the Royal Society for the Prevention of Accidents. The battery took 300 recharges through a domestic power point.

The inital plan was to sell the machine through mail order – then through electricity board showrooms, and finally through a supermarket chain. The C5's critics refused to take the project seriously, but Sinclair won support from prestige sports car makers Lotus. The unconventional vehicle, which used an adapted washing-machine motor, was built at the Hoover factory at Merthyr Tydfil in South Wales and was to be serviced by Hoover dealers.

Motoring experts were invited to test drive the machine, which was hailed on its launch day as 'an example of brilliant lateral thinking'. They discovered the pedals were useful when the battery ran flat up a steep hill, but most of them just felt embarrassed at being seen in the three-wheeler.

Initially, the Welsh factory turned out 2,000 trikes. Eventual production was targetted at 100,000. Then the problems started. Four days after the controversial launch, marketing consultant Guy Pearce drove the machine to work and found it would have been quicker by bike. He was left high and dry a mile from his Streatham office in London when the machine ran out of juice.

What should have been a quick, commuting trip from his Chelsea home – just four miles away – turned into an embarrassing journey during which Guy had to pedal furiously to get to work on time. 'At first,' said Guy, 'the trip was great fun. A lot of people were shouting and waving.' But when the trike came to a standstill, he was furious. Sinclair agreed to give him his money back.

151

The same day, Transport Minister, Lynda Chalker, told the House of Commons that the Road Research Laboratory was monitoring the safety aspects of the C5.

Four weeks later, enthusiastic purchasers of the C5 were not so ecstatic. Student Nicholas Botting was the first person to be arrested while driving the C5. He had gallantly offered to drive the vehicle, which a girlfriend had won at a St Valentine's Day raffle. 'I wasn't paralytic or sloshed, just a bit tipsy. I had a bit of trouble wiring up the battery so I just started pedalling along behind her car,' said Nicholas. 'But I sort of wobbled . . . and that's when I caught the attention of these policemen.'

They charged him with driving a tricycle while unfit through drink. Luckily, he was acquitted a couple of months later. Said Nicholas after his acquittal: 'I don't want anything more to do with the C5. It's quite a comic little thing isn't it? I wouldn't be seen in one again.'

By this time, motoring organizations such as the Automobile Association had aired reservations about Sinclair's cycle-cum-car. Richard Ballantine of *Bicycle Action* magazine tested the C5. His conclusion was: 'As a concept it is brilliant. As a vehicle it is nowhere.'

In March 1985, production of the C5 was halted. By this time, 5,000 of the C5s had been sold by mail order. But there were rumours that the revolutionary machine was in trouble. Sir Clive Sinclair had deferred a decision to invest up to £2 million in a second production line. The 1,700 workers at the Hoover plant in Wales had staged a one-day strike, called to coincide with a visit by the Prince and Princess of Wales, in protest against overtime.

Questions were being asked: was the little plastic pedal machine, aimed at bringing a bit of economic joy to London commuters, fun – or folly? Was the electric vehicle – unique but controversial – really a landmark in motoring history? Or were we better off with having just our 27,000 electric milk floats?

People still gave the C5 some benefit of doubt. There was still the fact that it was the first electric runabout. Sir Clive himself was surprised that demand for his creation was not greater. He blamed the press for lack of foresight and pessimistic reporting. A special team of teenage testers was recruited. Their job was to take the C5s around London to 'increase public awareness'. For a fee of £20 a day the teenagers drove and pedalled the Sinclair tricycle around the City and answered questions from curious passers-by.

Sir Clive attacked established motor manufacturers for holding back the development of the electric car to protect investments in the internal combustion engine. But his problems would not go away.

Sir Clive Sinclair before the C5's troubles began.

At least, the workers at Hoover went back to work. They accepted a four per cent pay offer, ended their two-month overtime ban and agreed to the company's £10m investment package which would modernise the factory. It would also mean up to 500 job losses.

There were further problems when it was decided more people in the world should have the benefit of a C5. Changes were needed to bring the vehicle in line with laws in Europe.

By October 1985, two receivers were called in by Sir Clive to sort out his troubled C5 car company. The news was even more dismal by November.

Sir Clive's dream of tomorrow's motoring became 'the ideal Christmas gift' at a special mark-down price of £139.99 (including VAT, the batteries and accessories).

The offer was made by Woolworth's, arm of the Comet Discount firm. It was a sad bargain. The original price had been slashed by 65 per cent.

What its harshest critics called 'that most useless of vehicles, the washing-machine motor-powered C5 trolley' did make a minor comeback three years after it drove into obscurity. Do-it-yourself enthusiast David Burton thought he was doing his sister a favour fitting a C5 engine to her baby's pram in hilly Exmouth, Devon. But the Department of Transport declared it illegal.

The final sad saga for the C5 became a desert song.

Oil-rich sheikhs could see its merits in a hot climate, where the rest of the world, it seemed, had not. Orders came flooding in from the Middle East, boosting business for Maurice Levensohn of Liverpool, who had snapped up the last 7,000 models to be made and sold them for £100 to the Sheiks.

They may have lost Sir Clive a fortune, but they made money for Maurice.

'I'll be keeping at least one C5 back as a collector's item,' he said.

Missile mistake

A Russian cruise missile flew dangerously off course after the wrong flight plan was put into its computer by mistake, and had to be shot down in Finland.

The missile was launched on December 28, 1985, from a frigate of the Soviet northern fleet on test trials in the Barents See, north of Norway. It was meant to land at the Russian's land testing site at Novazemia, but because of the accidental computer programming it headed for northern Norway.

The Russians immediately dispatched two MiG interceptors with pilots specially trained to shoot down cruise missiles. 'For God's sake, get it!' they were commanded. One of them did, complying with instructions to ensure it was done from within Soviet territory.

The missile had passed about two miles south east of Kirkenes, a busy airport in the north of Norway used by businesses with iron ore mining interests.

The missile, chased by the MiG 25, first climbed to 13,000 feet at 600 miles an hour.

It was first monitored going over a small Norwegian fishing village, Jakobsleve, then across Sholpen Bank, past Kirkenes and on towards Skogfoss, a village on the border between Norway and Russia. Though not armed with a conventional or nuclear warhead, experts later worked out from its speed and line of path that it was heading for Hamburg or Bremen, West Germany's two largest ports.

That was when the Russians really began to worry. They had just 25 minutes to stop the missile.

The MiG 25 jet pilot managed to hit the missile somewhere near Skogfoss. Most of the wreckage came to rest in Finland. Five weeks later, Finnish air force investigators were still finding bits. Finnish authorities clearly recognised Soviet lettering on the fallen pieces. But no-one in the area was officially given a reason for the 'supersonic boom' they heard that December morning.

The Finns issued an official statement that what had been found was Russian flight-testing equipment, even though witnesses on the ground described seeing a turbo jet thundering across the sky.

'The Finnish authorities did not want to upset the Russians by calling them liars.' Diplomacy was the wisest policy on this occasion.

The Soviet authorities had in fact immediately contacted the Pentagon to warn the Americans about the rogue missile.

Because arms control talks were due to begin in Geneva only ten days later, America asked Norway, into whose air space it had wandered, not to take action. The Soviet ambassador to Norway at the time, Dmitri Poliansky, conveyed a discreet message of apology to the Norwegians.

The decline and fall of the French emperor

Napoleon was at first a true and loyal leader of the French. His revolutionary slogan 'Liberty, Equality, Fraternity' which once echoed throughout Europe, was finally debased. The people of France had come to realize just what a tyrant Napoleon Bonaparte really was.

His obsession with conquest, dictatorship over a country which once revered him and an alliance between his enemies were to bring about his downfall. A decision to complete his empire-building by invading Russia in 1812, was the greatest military mistake he ever made. We must first look at the early days of the man who was to become master of most of Europe, to see into the mind of Napoleon.

Born at Ajaccio, the capital of Corsica, in 1769, Napoleon Bonaparte received a military education as a humble pensioner of the King of France. By 1792 he was a captain of artillery. The brilliance of his first fight with the English at the siege of Toulon in 1793 marked him out as the French Revolution's finest general. Within three years he was head of an army – helped along by his marriage to the influential Creole widow, Josephine de Beauharnais.

When in 1796, General Bonaparte launched his campaign against the Austrians in Italy, he was just 27. His rise had been meteoric.

Napoleon returned from his Italian triumphs to launch new schemes of conquest. He would conquer Egypt, turn the British out of India and crush the power of Turkey on his way back.

Napoleon's fatal weakness was that he always underestimated the strength of England and the importance of sea power. ('The Channel is a ditch which it needs but a little courage to cross,' he once boasted.) His victories in the Egyptian expedition of 1797-98 were nullified by Nelson's destruction of the French fleet in Aboukir Bay – the Battle of the Nile – and by an unsuccessful siege of Acre – 'The key of Constantinople or of India' Napoleon once confided to a companion.

Napoleon returned to France at an opportune moment. The currents of the Revolution needed direction. Anarchy threatened and a second coalition had been formed by the enemies of France, whose armies had many able captains but lacked a master mind. Napoleon, assisted by his grenadiers, seized the reins of civil power, became First Consul and made his home in the magnificent palace of the Tuileries. It was only a short time before his next move for conquest. Crossing the Alps with an army of 40,000 men, he launched a lightning strike against the Austrians who were advancing in Italy and overthrew them at Marengo in June 1800.

In 1802, the Treaty of Amiens temporarily ended hostilities between England and France. But a year later, war between the two countries broke out again. Napoleon plunged into battle, both political and military. He made himself Emperor of France and from 1805 to 1814, led the French armies in a series of campaigns in many of which he displayed the soldier's supreme genius.

Napoleon's aggressive policy alarmed the rulers of Europe for he had annexed territory and established control in northern Italy. Again, he had to face a European coalition backed by Britain with ships, money and men. His plans for invasion of Britain were wiped out by Horatio Nelson's victory over a combined French and Spanish fleet at Trafalgar in 1805. Napoleon broke up his camp at Boulogne where intense preparations had been made for crossing to "perfidious Albion" and marched across Austria.

At Austerlitz in 1805, the emperor won a victory which caused British prime minister William Pitt to say: 'Roll up that map of Europe. It will not be wanted for ten years.' But Europe was in arms against the conqueror. Prussia mobilized for war and paid for it dearly. Her armies were overwhelmed at Jena and Avestadt in 1806 and Napoleon entered Berlin in triumph. He concluded the Treaty of Tilsit, which reduced Prussia to the position of a conquered state.

Napoleon's next move was not so victorious. He captured Madrid and left his brother Joseph to rule as king. The Spanish began to join in the hate-campaign against Napoleon.

In 1809, Austria collected her forces for another blow against the conquering Corsican. But Napoleon triumphed once more with a victory at Wagram.

By 1811, Napoleon was at the height of his power. So long as Russia remained his ally, he was virtually master of Europe. But the 'continental system' by which Napoleon sought to close every European port against the goods of his relentless enemy, Britain, began to break down. The French were deprived of cheap British textiles, of such comforts as coffee, sugar and tobacco. There was heavy French taxation and the requisitioning or commandeering of food and other stores.

The people of Europe were disillusioned. They recognized Napoleon for what he really was – a ruthless, power-crazy dictator – and they were more ready to support their rulers whole-heartedly in fighting the French.

More importantly, the Russian Tsar, Alexander, broke away from the imposed economic bondage and thus brought about the fatal rupture which ended with Napoleon's great invasion of Russia in 1812. The more cautious of his ministers frowned upon the invasion project. 'He will ruin us all,' Admiral Decres told a friend.

Napoleon paid no heed. He assembled a mixed army of 600,000 men and set forth to conquer Russia. His idea was to 'melt the states of Europe into one nation'. The Russians had their own, softly, softly campaign. They would draw the invaders deeper and deeper into a country deliberately left barren of supplies or stores – and encourage defeat through sheer exhaustion and absence of resources.

When Napoleon reached Russia he found a bitterly cold and hostile environment. There was nothing for him to seize to ease the fatigue of his soldiers. There were no people to be bullied into co-operation. And the cold! It tore an icy cut through the French soldiers' inadequate uniforms. But worse was to come. The army marched on to Moscow. Although the city was home to a quarter of a million people, it was virtually deserted! A fire broke out around midnight, waking the weary men. They beat out the fire, but then another broke out, and then another. The Russians' careful, calculated campaign to break the back of the French army was working well!

Napoleon waited for weeks, expecting Tsar Alexander to approach him to talk of peace. No word came. The weather got colder, supplies totally ran out, the men ailed. Reluctantly, the crushed conqueror decided to retreat. But he had left it far too late. The French army, perpetually harassed by the Cossacks, was caught in the iron grip of winter. As they tried to cross the Beresina, the conditions were so appalling, many died there and then.

Napoleon in a blue study.

From Napoleon's original Grand Army of 600,000, only 1,000 emaciated figures came back from the Russian wilderness. Apart from the appalling numbers of the dead, Napoleon suffered losses of about 3,000 soldiers, who deserted or stayed behind as prisoners. It is said that Napoleon's heroic Marshal Ney, ragged, dirty and blood-stained, staggered into the town hall of a border town and when asked who he was, shouted: 'I am the Grand Army!'

This ruinous campaign gave heart to the allies. It was followed by a revival of the coalition against Napoleon. Austria, Prussia and Sweden joined forces with the Russians. Overtures for peace were made. But the emperor would not listen. The French were defeated at Leipzig, the 'Battle of the Nations', in 1813. In the spring of 1814, Napoleon was forced to abdicate.

You would think that was the end of his ambitions for conquest. But on March 1st, 1815, Napoleon returned to the south of France with a few hundred soldiers. The famous Hundred Days began that were to end on June 18 – at Waterloo. Austrians, Russians, Germans and British were assembled ready to move towards the French frontier. Soon the news of Napoleon's defeat reached Paris.

Napoleon was still ranting about raising more men, more weapons. But enough was enough. France's ministers convened and when Napoleon joined them he discovered he was no longer in charge of France's destiny. The people wanted no more fighting. He offered to abdicate. The offer was accepted the very next day.

On June 22, 1815, Napoleon ceased to be emperor. He was banished to St Helena, an island off the west coast of Africa. Napoleon died of cancer six years later.

The man who wanted to rule Europe, instead turned his country against himself and died a lonely figure.